Before I begin; I just want to say a quick thank you to
To Joe Kruger for his contributions in this book. TO Bu Oats White,
our paranormal gadget guy and to Cerisia Ta Torin for the book cover.
And of course, to the many spirits, ghosts and energies who, without them
this book would never have happened.

AN ALPHABET OF SPOOKS

Intro

As a child I grew up in a convoluted family. On my mother's side were mediums and witches. My father's side were Irish Catholics.

So, this is how my life went on a weekly basis. On schooldays I would attend The Immaculate Mary convent. Now you might think that the nuns, being brides of Christ would be lovely creatures. Far from it. With their pinched faces and vinegary personalities, they were sarcastic, spiteful and cruel. Grade A bitches is MY best description.

The priest was worse though. I hated mass. It terrified me. I remember sitting and listening to his Hell and brimstone threats. I can remember thinking that I would definitely be going into spend eternity with Lucifer, because I was such a sinful, wicked child. To say that as a girl I was God fearing was an understatement.

As years went by though and I became older, (about eight I think), some of the Priests tales of terror, rather than frightening me, started to sow the seeds of doubt. I remember it was Ash Wednesday. I hated that day, when the nuns would smear oily ash on our foreheads. As usual the priest was spewing his usual bile, when suddenly it struck me that in one breath, he was threatening everlasting Hell and punishment, and in the next he gushed "God is love."

It was like a light came on for me. I remember thinking that God couldn't possibly be a terrifying ogre and a loving father both at the same time. This was all threats and lies, and in that moment, I was cured of religion.

By total contrast the weekends were a vastly different barrel of fish.

On Friday nights Mum and me would go to grandma's house. My aunt Sandy would be there too. I wasn't allowed to join in because I was too young, so I would sit on the sofa and watch as the women of my family started to prepare for the circle.

They would light candles and clean a small, round wooden table. Next, they spread letters that were drawn on stiff white card around its edges. This was how Ouija boards used to look before Waddington turned them into a game. Then a small sparkling, crystal shot glass was blessed and set in the centre of the table.

Shortly after there would be a roar of motorcycle engines as members of our gathering arrived. Remember now, this was back in the 60's. No crash helmets were worn. The guys mostly wore studded leather jackets, and the women has hair styles like Marilyn Monroe, or Myra Hindley.

Once everyone was seated grandma would open the circle. Fingers were placed upon the upturned glass and moments later it started to spin. Moving slowly at first and then gathering momentum as the energy grew, deceased loved ones and spirit guides used the board to spell out messages. Although this was a regular meeting, the heartfelt communications from familiar spirits were always comforting and spellbinding.

It wasn't just Ouija boards and messages that kept grandmas gathering well attended. All sorts of weird and wonderful things happened during these evenings. I remember on one occasion the glass suddenly shattered and as it did, we saw that one of the circle, a slim fair-haired biker called Jimmy, started to go into trance. His breathing became shallow, his eyes rolled back in his head and then closed. Then slowly the face of a ghostly stranger started to transfigure over his own. The spirit was using the energy from the circle to transfigure. A luminescent grey mist seemed to ooze from Jimmys solar plexus. Rising up it morphed into a mask-like image of a Sikh with a silk turban. The visitants' eyes glinted dark as it gazed around the room. There were many nights like that, and as I grew up paranormal experiences because normal (but still fascinating) to me.

Unsurprisingly I suppose, my connection to the spirit world started to develop at an early age. I was interested in all forms of divination. My Aunt Sandy mentored me in the use of tarot cards and tealeaf reading. (A skill handed down from my Great-Grandmother), so from 14 years of age, I was a competent medium and card reader. It was then that I became the local oracle, mostly for teen friends who wanted to know about possible romance in their lives, and although over the years me reputation grew as an accurate clairvoyant, I never thought of it as my path. I was just something that I could do.

In February 2000 that was to change as my Invisible Friend Richard came into my life and turned everything upside down. (I'll share more about that later in this book) and together we've worked all over the UK as well as Australia, Norway and many other countries. Our story and work have been featured in many international magazines, such as Australia's Universal Mind. Prediction and Kindred Spirit in the UK and in Norway's two top spiritual publications Medium and Magic.

Whilst working as a professional medium I often share my supernatural experiences, and I have been asked many times when I'm going to write a book about my many encounters with Ghosts.

I guess this is the moment when I decided to crack on with it. (As we say in Cornwall). So I decided to write my A to Z of spooks.

A is for Animals;

I am often asked about pets in the afterlife. Anyone who has loved and lost a special furry friend knows that it can be just as painful as the loss of any human loved one. Pets are family too and the rainbow bridge is absolutely real. Here are a couple of stories. Both of a doggy nature.

One gloomy October morning I was waiting in a long queue in my local GP's surgery to collect a prescription. The surgery is in Marazion, a pretty little village which dates back to the 1500's. It's most famous for St Michaels Mount and is a popular holiday destination, but many of the classic Cornish cottages now belong to "posh people".

So, I'm in the queue looking a bit rustic as is my way, standing in line with mostly conservative looking people all sensibly dressed, when in walks an older lady who looks like she's just stepped off the front cover of "Country Life". She's now standing just behind me when, out of my peripheral vision I notice the spirit of a Springer Spaniel right next to her wagging its tail and looking from me to her all excitedly. Now this was not the time or place to be giving out clairvoyant messages. In all directions I'm surrounded by very straight looking people, not to mention fearsome GP receptionists (and we all know what they can be like). But looking down I can still see this little dog, tongue lolling out, eyes shining, full of enthusiasm. Now anyone who has ever owned a dog will know the psychological pressure they can apply when pestering you to do something. Spirit dogs are no different. So, I realise that I have no choice but to bite the bullet. I turn to the lady and say "You'll probably think I've got a screw loose but I'm a medium and when you walked in you had a little Springer Spaniel with you. Does that make any sense?" (I could feel the queue of straights shifting uncomfortably). She gasped and quietly replied "No, that's okay, what colour is it?" I told her that the dog was liver and white. I could see she was struggling to hold her emotions in check. "I lost him two weeks ago" she whispered. "The house is so empty without him" She thanked me for passing on the message and I could see in her smile that it brought her some comfort to know that her pet was still nearby, I was very glad that I plucked up the courage to deliver the doggy message. It made me chuckle to think of the captive audience who couldn't have failed to overhear what happened. I wonder what they made of it?

Food for thought, I'm sure.

My second story is very similar, but I'll tell it just the same. Occasionally, as well as my psychic work, I take a part time job. On this occasion I was helping at a friend's village store and petrol station. Looking out of the window I noticed a brightly coloured VW camper van pull up. A young couple jumped out and the guy started to fill up with fuel while the girl came in and wandered around picking up provisions.

As she started towards the checkout, I became aware of a ball of grey energy, following along besides her with a trundling motion. (WTF?) The nearer she got, the more solid the energy became until by the time she stood in front of me it had manifested into the sturdy shape of a little silver Staffie.

Now I have this belief that if a spirit of any type is trying hard to get your attention, and if you're lucky enough to have the ability, then it's your duty to deliver the message. So here we go again "You're probably going to think I'm nuts" (The girl looks bewildered). "This isn't my main job. I work as a medium. Did you ever have a little silver Staffie? Stunned, she nodded at me, eyes wide. "Well, he came into the shop with you. He walks like a little wrestler" The girl's eyes filled with tears. She rushed out of the shop.

I was just beginning to think that I should have kept my mouth shut, when she returned with her partner. "I can't believe it" she says through the tears "That's Bruno, we lost him last week. We had to have him put down because he had cancer of the nose"

They were both so happy to know that their beloved boy was still with them. It turned out that they were both very much on their spiritual pathway. They had recently started going to Mind, Body & Spirit festivals and were both studying Reiki.

So, the story goes "A dog is not just for Christmas. It's for life" - actually, if it's soulmate dog, it's for ever, and will keep you company through many incarnations.

My third story is a non-doggy one. While working at an event in Newport in Wales a lady came up to my table for a reading. Everything was going along well, with loved ones from Spirit coming in with messages. Suddenly, I could see clairvoyantly, what looked like a dark turret. Then slowly manifesting out of the shadows, I saw a little brown pony. (WTF?). Although the image was confusing, I felt very strongly that I needed to reassure my client that the pony was okay now.

After some thought I told my client what I had been shown, and asked if it made any sense. Her expression started to change. She looked down. Sadly, she explained to me that she had owned the little bay pony called Robin. He had been with the family for years and was much loved. Although he was well cared for, he had been in the same field for several years and it had been grazed bare.

Then one day a new neighbour who had recently moved to the village into a smallholding asked if the pony would like some fresh grazing? Gladly she had jumped at the offer, excited for her pony to have better grass.

The next day she took her little pony to the field, took off his headcollar and watched as he galloped off, bucking and kicking in excitement.

Every day she would go and check on him, take a bucket of feed and give him a groom, everything was going well, but then about a week later, she had gone to the field as usual, but she couldn't see him anywhere.

She walked around, checking the fences but all the boundaries were secure. Then she heard a faint whinny, but she couldn't make out where it was coming from. It seemed to come from a clump of bracken and gorse in the corner of the paddock.

She ran over and calling to him, the pony cried out in reply, and then she saw it and her heart broke. Obscured by the foliage was a deep dark hole. Sadly, unknown to anyone, amongst the brambles was an uncapped mine shaft and the pony had fallen in.

The vet, police and fire brigade were called but despite their best efforts the pony could not be saved. My client sat with tears in her eyes. Head bowed.

Then in my mind I saw the pony swish his tail, put in a massive buck and then gallop off into a beautiful flower filled meadow. In his own way Robin was showing me that he was free, and he didn't want his to be sad anymore. He was over the rainbow bridge where all pets and animals go, and he was happy.

Over the years I have had so many animal companions come through during readings to let their owners know that they're still with them. Cats, dogs, rabbits, ponies, all sorts, even an elephant once. The rainbow bridge is a real place and all the pets that you have loved and lost will be there waiting for you when your time comes to cross over, and that's just as well.

How boring would the afterlife be if there were no animals?

B is for Blue Anchor:

Among other things, Cornwall is known for its many very ancient pubs. The Blue Anchor is one of the very oldest, dating back to the 15th century, and famous for its home brewed beer called Spingo. (Which should be served with a public health warning).

The Blue is just as you might imagine. A rickety cottage style building with low doorways and ceilings. (The Cornish were shorter back in the day). The bar, chairs and tables are rustic and worn by the elbows and bums of many a thirsty traveller. Out the back is a skittle alley and walled beer garden.

The Blue is also said to be very haunted.

One evening I was there with a friend. We were waiting for my son's band to finish a gig. So, we ordered a pint and sat by the window at a big, dark oak wood table.

I was leaning back into my chair, at an arm's length from the table, just relaxing, when suddenly, my pint (which I hadn't touched) lifted into the air and launched itself into my lap, drenching me with beer. (Why does poltergeist activity never happen when you're filming?)

A young couple sitting across from me looked horrified and hurriedly got up and left, but an old local in the corner bust out laughing and said "That always happens if someone sits in that chair"

Even though I was drenched and smelled like a brewery, I was absolutely blown away by what had happened. Obviously a long dead local was still hanging around, longing for a drink, and clearly resenting anyone who sat in HIS chair enjoying a pint.

(It's worth saying too that anyone who is interested in paranormal activity could do much worse than to check out old pubs. Over the centuries they've been a meeting place for all sorts of shenanigans, and very many spooks like to return there to remember good times, or to settle old scores.

The Blue Anchor has always had a reputation for being haunted and I have another story to tell.

When I am teaching mediumship, I like to take students on location. This particular night we had chosen The Blue. I had arrived early and was waiting for my group to arrive.

At this point I must digress to make the story understandable. Back in the 1980s I ran an equine rescue centre. I would take in horses and ponies that had been abused or that were just dumped because they were old and sick. The Sanctuary was called Nags End.

Over the years Nags End collected a lot of supporters. One of them was Alex. Alex was a gypsy and a local character. Everybody locally knew him or at least who he was. He lived in a traditional barrel caravan which was pulled by a massive black and white cob called Sam. (Sam was well known for being unpredictable).

So anyway, on this evening I am waiting at the bar for my group to arrive when in walks Alex. "Hello Angie" he beamed "I haven't seen you for a long time. Do you still have the horses?" We struck up a conversation. It was good to see him after so long. As we chatted, I couldn't help noticing how well he looked. His skin looked fresh and bright. His checked shirt and jeans looked new, and even his weird hat looked like it had been in the washing machine. I was really pleased that he was obviously doing well.

Then along came my students so Alex and I said our goodbyes and I went off to run my circle.

Later on, that evening when I got back to my lodgings (I was sofa surfing at the time) I remarked to my friend who was putting me up, that I had bumped into Alex. I told her that he had looked really well and that it had been so good to catch up. My friend looked at me as if I was loopy. "But Alex is dead," She cried. He died quite a while ago. I thought that she must be wrong. "But I stood talking to him," I explained. "He was as real as I was".

We hit Google, and there it was. Alex' death had made the Westcountry papers because he had been such a local treasure.

The Blue Anchor had been a favourite of his. I guess he had dropped in because he sensed that I was visiting. It was crazy that I had seen him so clearly. I never could have known that he was a ghost.

If you visit Helston in Cornwall at any point. It's well worth dropping in for a pint of Spingo, because you never know who you might meet there.

C is for Charlotte:

It was my son Joe who suggested we visit a monument that stood at the edge of Bodmin moor, under the shadow of Rough Tor.

Whilst researching he had come across the story of Charlotte Diamond. She had been a local girl who was murdered 200 years ago, and whose body had been found floating in a stream under an ancient bronze age bridge. Her throat cut.

Way back then the community would have been very isolated being out on the edge of the moorlands. So, something as horrible as the murder of a young girl would have been extra shocking for the locals. Shortly after she was found dead the people from her village erected a stone monument in her memory. It stands by the stream where she was found in a very bleak and barren landscape.

It didn't take the local police long to discover that her boyfriend had been the murderer. Apparently, he had become jealous because another local lad had been showing interest. Although he denied the charges, there was a lot of incriminating evidence against him, so he was eventually arrested, charged and then hanged at the infamous Bodmin jail.

On the anniversary of Charlotte's death, Joe and I drove out to find her monument. We didn't know what to expect. After much wading through and around marshland and climbing over granite boulders we arrived at the spot.

When we arrived were surprised to see that others had been there before us, as fresh flowers had been left. Garlands of roses, iris and lilies lay around the granite base, petals fluttering in the breeze like butterfly wings. It seemed that Charlotte's story had touched a lot of people who had taken the time to visit her stone and remember her.

Joe took out his K2 and we followed the stream along to the bridge. The ancient bridge with its large, flat time-worn granite stones must have transported countless footsteps over the spot where poor Charlottes body had lay undiscovered. The gurgling water with and steep moss lined riverbank must have been much the same as back then on the day that she was slain. The nearer we got, the more the K2 lit up. But then something unexpected happened. The energy started to change, there was a shift and as we started to feel Charlotte's energy.

From having read her story one would imagine a feeling of fear or sorrow, but far from being sad or lost her energy felt happy, excited. Joyful even. Joe's K2 was going crazy flashing from red to green and back again. He stooped down to look under the bridge, and as he did, I heard her say in a strong Cornish accent "Hello my angel."

Not only was she at peace, but she was thrilled and excited that people had taken the time to visit her on her anniversary. It was a lovely experience, and both of us were buzzing from it for the whole drive home.

We have decided to visit on her anniversary this year again and will leave flowers for her. She is such a lovely little soul.

D is for Differences;

Okay, I was stretching my alphabet a bit with this one, but this is a huge subject. I want to talk about the difference between the various supernatural energies.

An important part of my work is helping people to remove visiting or haunting entities from their homes or other buildings. It helps a lot if you know exactly what you're dealing with.

There's quite a big difference between the likes of Ghosts and Poltergeists etc. I'll give you a few examples to illustrate the difference.

On one occasion I was asked to a house where there had been poltergeist activity. It had been bought by a young couple called Jan and Freddy Jones.

At all times, night or day, lights were being turned off and the TV and Radio were being turned on. There was generally a lot of activity around electrical devices in the home.

The couple had only recently moved into the house. They were first time buyers and had been excited to be able to finally get their own home. Money had been a struggle but finally they had managed to save a little, so this was a big moment for them.

The house itself was old and shabby and needed a lot of work. So, they had moved in, rolled up their sleeves and made a start.

Everything needed re-doing. Wallpaper had to be stripped. Paint rubbed down and refreshed. The kitchen cupboards needed to come out, pretty much everything. The young couple were using every spare moment that they had, in-between working to forge ahead with their DIY. However, something weird started to happen.

The main activity was focused on the living room and kitchen. Often when they would settle down for the evening, tired after a busy day. Suddenly all the lights would turn off and the TV channels would start to switch around, flicking from one station to another.

Now one thing you really don't need when you're unfamiliar with anything paranormal is to think you might have a Ghost suddenly plunging you into darkness, especially when you're tired and just want to chill.

Then there was the kitchen. The young couple would switch on the kettle or turn on a cooker hob on – only to see the devices be turned back off by an unseen hand right in front of their eyes. "Click"

Although Jan and Freddy weren't into the supernatural as such, they had an open mind on the subject – but this experience had cleared up any doubts as to whether Spooks existed, and they were getting jumpy. They were worried in case they had something nasty trying to drive them from their home. So they decided to look for help. They called their local Spiritualist Centre who suggested that they contact me.

Whenever I'm asked to move a Spirit on, I always start with trying to communicate with them. In my opinion rushing in reciting prayers and burning sage can often make things worse.

Imagine if you were really upset about something but your worries were ignored, and instead of getting support you were pushed out into the cold. That's how it must feel to a confused and emotional spirit. Trying to talk about things at least has the chance of helping, just as it would with any troubled person.

So, I arrived at their home. It was an old, terraced house on the outskirts of Redruth. It was one of the old miners' cottages and about 200 years old. As soon as I am invited inside, I can feel a presence. It's doesn't feel dark though.

I walk around burning sage. Not to dispel the spirit, but to relax and quieten the mood. I start by asking if there is anything that I can do to help and ask if the spirit is okay. (At this point I felt an older male come in).

I enquire if this had been his home? I feel a tingle. It had. I felt as if he was unhappy about the renovations, so I explained that this was done to take care of the house and add that it would be lovely if it could become a family home again. I talked about how the house might feel at special times like Christmas, with the open fire ablaze, children chatting excitedly and the smell of a big roast dinner cooking. Did he remember things like that? The energy shifted.

I then gently asked if the Spirit knew that he had died? (My strong point is clairaudience). He seemed unsure. I talked to him about how his loved ones in the Spirit World would be missing him and how maybe he should go and have a catch up. I then heard the name, Roger.

At this point Jan and Freddi looked agog. Roger was the name of the previous owner. He had lived alone in the house after his wife had passed, and sadly he had died alone in the house at the age of 92.

It seemed that as Roger was used to living alone that he had just stayed behind after his death. It must have felt normal to him. Now Jan and Freddie knew who their lodger was, they were much less afraid. Jan then did a brilliant thing. She explained to Roger that they only wanted to care for the house and that he would be welcome to come and visit to see how the improvements and repairs were going on. I felt the energy change.

Roger was at peace and was ready to go into the light to join his wife. He was happy that Jan had promised to look after the house that he had been so fond of and that he could come back whenever he wanted to see the work that had been done.

As the energy became lighter, I clearly heard Roger say, "Can you thank them for me please, but would you ask if I can still come to watch the cricket on TV when I visit?"

It turned out that was why he was turning the radio and TV on and scrolling through the channels. He was looking for the cricket games and results. He had also been worried about his energy bills when he was on the earth, so that's why he was turning off the lights and cooker rings.

By the end of my visit Roger had happily gone to the Spirit World to catch up with his family. I spoke to Jan and Freddy a few months later. They said that house was much quieter now, but that sometimes that they could feel him around. Also, whenever they were going out, they left the radio or TV on if there was a cricket match – Just in case.

Roger was a Spirit. Spirits are people who have passed over and are very much themselves. They can communicate and know what is happening in real time (Our real time).

A Ghost is different – Here's another story.

As I wander around the UK and abroad doing my work, I often stay in hotels. One that I have stayed in many times is the George and Pilgrim in Glastonbury.

As many of you will know, the G&P is very well known for being haunted. I've written about it before in my other book "Diary of a Trance Medium"

This time I was travelling with another medium, Nicki Honey.

When we arrived there had been a mix up with our bookings, so instead of having two singles we were put in the big family room.

There were three beds. Two singles and a double. One single is at the far end of the room and the two other beds are near the window at the other end.

After dinner we settle down for the night. Nikki is in the double bed and I'm in the single at the far end of the room.

Now I'm an insomniac at the best of times, but this is something else. I get comfortable and start to try to sleep, but there is an energy hovering around. It's heavy and intense. I toss and turn and then open my eyes.

Overhead I can see swirls of black smoke in the darkness (I have seen this before with darker spirits). Sometimes it happens as an expression of the emotions that the entity is expressing. Anger or rage becoming visual.

As I'm beginning to realise what's going on I suddenly see an angry male face peering out of the smoke. The face is a pale grey, the colour of storm clouds. His jaw is tense, nostrils flared. With a furrowed brow and eyes scrunched he peered at me and scowled.

Instantly my brow chakra activates making my head spin, and clairvoyantly I can see a bare-knuckle fighter standing in a boxing ring in a dingy, underground cellar. It's obviously an illegal fight. He's dripping with sweat and bleeding from his nose as he lands heavy blows on his opponent.

Then I can feel him in the room. He's pacing, menacing and angry. I'll never get any sleep in this bed I complain. "What's going on?" Asks Nikki. " I have to change beds. There is an angry ghost at this end" I explain.

I try to talk to him, but his energy is raging. He is pacing backwards and forwards, but only to halfway across the room. I notice too that he is floating above the floor.

It is obvious that he is a Ghost, caught in the moment. He thinks that the room was the same as when he died there. There would have been a wall, which is why he doesn't move towards the window and the floor must have dropped over time, which is why he floats above it. He is caught in the moment, full of anger.

I tried my best to talk to him and offered help, but there was nothing I could do. I just couldn't reach him. It was getting late, and his energy was beginning to make me feel sick, I had no choice but to move to the other end of the room and to leave him to it.

Because he was a Ghost it would be very difficult (but not impossible) for us to help him and probably would have taken a great deal of time. Ghosts are caught in a loop. Whatever happened to them at the point of passing, has got them so fixated that that is all they see.

My Invisible friend Richard tells me that ghosts are like the heavily sedated patients in a Victorian Asylum. They are so foggy that only that moment exists. It's very sad.

After I had changed beds, the fighter didn't bother me again, and I managed to get some sleep.

So, those are the two main types, Ghosts and Spirits, but there are many others. I could have written this whole book on the subject.

Another phenomenon which is worth mentioning, because it's not uncommon, is the creation of an entity from human intention, actions and conjurings. Maybe you've heard that "thought" is a living energy? Thought is the active component in Magic, Absent Healing, Witchcraft, Voodoo and many other practices.

On several occasions I have been asked to a home that is allegedly haunted, but when I get there however it's technically not. Although there is an energy present.

It's difficult to know how to explain this. Sometimes in an environment where there is anger, violence, fear or sometimes addiction, the residents give off their own energy and it collects. I suppose it's very similar to residual energy, where echoes of trauma soak into the fibre of a building and create an atmosphere. However, in this case the entity that is created isn't bound to the structure of a building, it has a body, a form, but no capacity to think. I guess these entities are somewhat like the old zombies that you might see in a TV series like "The Walking Dead" - they are there. They appear human – but there is nothing beyond that.

In cases such as these it's possible to clear the entity with sage and salt. However, if things don't improve then they will form again. In this situation it's the living people who need to be healed. Issues with anger need resolving, addictions need to be healed and the home it's self needs to be spring cleaned and cared for.

A loved and happy home can go a long way to help raise the energy of both living people and those who have passed.

E is for Entity

There are all sorts of Spirits beings and generally they are just the same as most incarnated people. Perfectly reasonable, friendly and helpful, but as with everyday people, not all of them.

My Invisible Friend (Richard) tells me that everyone and everything, has at its core an essential light. (From God, the Universe whatever you want to call it). However, as some individuals evolve, sometimes because of their life experiences, they become dark, twisted or bitter, and that is what can create an entity or dark spirit.

I guess it's much the same as the theory that the abused become the abusers.

Now as part of my work I have encountered quite a few Dark Spirits. As I said in my intro though, If I wrote about all of them then this book would never get finished. So, I've chosen just one story here – it has all the classic features of a malevolent entity.

I have already talked about lost souls and how I always try to communicate with a Ghost of Spirit that is upset or stuck.

There is no point trying to clear a spirit who has unfinished business, or you will just make them panic and they will cling more. These things must be worked through empathically. It's the same as having a counsellor on the earth really. Understanding brings healing and then the client can move forward

With Spirits, when you are well practiced you can feel what sort of energy you are connecting to, and although they may have a powerful energy that's sometimes difficult to deal with, it is nothing compared to an energy that is dark.

With distressed spirits you may feel an overwhelming sense of sorrow. You may feel great waves of emotion, and these might feel very strong. These sensations won't be yours; they will be coming from the Spirit as it tries to show you how it is feeling. That's all just part of mediumship and is quite normal.

The energy from an entity or Dark Spirit is something entirely different – and it's unmistakable. Often a room where an entity resides will have a chill. Occasionally there will be a smell of damp or a peppery odour. (If the entity is demonic, you may smell sulphur) The other thing that is very obvious with dark spirits is the physical feeling that you will get, and that feels almost like a punch in the gut. It's as if the darkness goes right to your very core. It's an unmistakable feeling, the sensation is very primal.

So to my story now. My Son Joe is also a Paranormal Investigator and has had a lot of experience with Spirits of a darker nature.

On this occasion the appointment was his, but he asked for my opinion on it.

Joe was contacted by a young single Mum called Laura and asked if he would go to her house as she was sure that she had something nasty going on energetically.

He told me that as soon as he walked into the building, he could feel a very heavy oppressive presence watching him.

Joe works with sound to clear haunted places. He is a musician so understands how sound works. It's not my area, but I do know that it's something to do with the resonance. When particular frequencies are played the vibrations can permeate both matter and energy and the oscillation clears blockages or residual energy.

On this occasion Joe had used salt in the corners of the house (so that the entity wouldn't be able to hide there). Then he burned sage and used tingshas to attempt to lift the energy. (A Tingsha is a pair of small Tibetan cymbals joined by a leather strap; they have a very high frequency).

Joe walked around as the chimes rang out, but the energy stayed very fixed and unsettling. There were places around the house that felt ominous. He said that when he stood at the top of the stairs, the atmosphere felt so strong that he expected to feel a push as he walked down them. Joe explains "It's important to mentally stand your ground when trying to clear negative entities. They will want you to feel like you can't go to some places, like you are not welcome or that it would be dangerous"

When he is working and finds a spot where the energy is very fixed and confrontational Joe likes to stand there a while. He talks to the entity and tries, at least to explain that it needs to leave. He says, "It's important too that you don't allow fear to overwhelm you, or at least that if you are fearful, you don't show it".

After assessing the situation at Laura's house, he went downstairs to share his findings. As they were talking, suddenly they heard footsteps moving along the length of the upstairs floor, but there was no one else in the house. Then several things happened in quick succession.

The vinyl floor in the adjoining room started creaking as if under tremendous pressure from a heavy weight. Joe raced into the hall to check out what was happening but as he did so was distracted by a cacophony of rumblings, rattling and eerie sounds coming from Laura's son's bedroom above. They raced upstairs only to find all the battery powered toys had been activated and were whizzing around the room. All of this was very classic poltergeist activity. This Entity meant business, and this was a show of strength. It was clear to Joe that this was going to take some time to deal with.

Later that day Joe called me, and I offered to go over myself the next day and see what I picked up.

That evening as I got ready for bed, I felt unsettled. There was no reason why. Shrugging it off I showered, made hot chocolate and then settled down for the night. I drifted off.

Now Medical people put anything weird that happens at night as "Night Terrors or Sleep Paralysis. Those of us that are experienced in the paranormal know that not all those things are generated by a troubled mind and there are big differences between those sleep paralysis and psychic attacks.

Another thing that is worth mentioning here (I'm trying not to go too off track) is that when you are in an in-between state (not quite asleep and not quite awake) your mind is in the perfect state to be able to see and hear supernatural beings. At that time all your mediumistic abilities are enhanced. Even more-so around 3am in the morning.

In my hazy state I start to sense that there is something in my room. I try to wake up, but my head is woozy, as if I've had one to many. I'm struggling now to force myself awake and begin to come to. My mind is clearing now but I can't move or speak. I recognise what's happening, I've had this before.

Very strong entities can paralyse you with their mind. They mess with your head and can make it very difficult to think clearly. I have learned over the years though that in these situations the thing to do is not to panic (Yeah, I know that sounds tricky). It you show fear or anger a negative spirit can feed from those emotions to become stronger – you must stay neutral to take away their power.

My head is clearer now, and I begin to be able to function. I open my eyes and immediately see that the ceiling of my room is obscured by a swirling grey mist. Slowly the mist parts and a beautiful face starts to emerge. Almond shaped eyes, reflective like mirrors. High cheekbones and a perfect jawline. Androgynous as many entities and angles tend to be. but despite its appearance the energy that it exudes was very dark.

Then the Entity spoke with a mocking tone. (It's very common for Spirits of this kind to try and mess with your head and attack your vulnerabilities) "It really is a dreadful shame that your father never really cared about you, isn't it? Well, he's dead now anyway, so he's not here to save you. I doubt that he would have bothered even if he could. You really were a pointless and dull child"

Then a weird thing happened (Yes even weirder). Although I was in my bedroom with the door shut, I could see out into the garden. There shambling up the path were half a dozen wraith-like spirits trudging towards my back door. Dishevelled and ragged, they looked like zombies. Each of them held old farm tools, Scythes, shovels, pitch forks that glinted in the moonlight. They were coming to get me. I had no doubt about that. I centred myself and focused my mind preparing to resist the attack.

Then I remembered the demon's taunts. It had tried to find my weaknesses to intimidate me, trying to make my mind weak, however it had got me wrong. Although my relationship with my father had been difficult, I had dealt with any negative memories. There was no purchase to be had here.

I sat up in bed and spoke to the Entity. In an assertive manner I told it that it had underestimated me, the things that it said couldn't hurt me or make me weak and that it had no power over me, and neither did its henchmen. I felt its energy shift as my mind strengthened. I then visualised a ball of brilliant white light that was getting bigger and bigger, pushing all spirits back. I held that image for a while whilst reciting the Lord's Prayer. There was a momentary stalemate, a feeling of hovering and then the energy became calm, and the spirits disappeared.

Obviously, the Entity didn't like that I was going to visit Laura's home in the morning and had tried to put me off.

The next day Joe and I both went to do cleansings on the house in using our own individual methods and Joe returned for a few more sessions after which we were told that the energy had improved, and the paranormal activity was much less.

We are not sure what brought the entity to Laura's home. It's not always clear how these things happen. I'm just glad that on this occasion we were able to help.

F is for Fairies;

There are so many supernatural beings. It's not just Spirits and Angels. Every living thing has an essence, trees, flowers, water, stones (Yes Water and Stones are a living energy).

One of my fascinations has always been the Unseelie Court. These are a band of darkly inclined fairies; they are known for their mischievous and sometimes cruel behaviour especially towards humans.
They are particularly known for ambushing hikers and folks that wander off into the woods or moors alone. Especially if they lay down to rest. The Unseelie Courts are said to capture these unlucky travellers and spirit them away to goodness knows where, never to return.
It's true that an awful lot of people go missing all around the world and I'm sure that's often due to misadventure, but who's to say some of them aren't kidnapped by the Fairies?

As part of this journey that I'm on with my Invisible Friend I/We have been lucky enough to work in many countries overseas. One place where I've worked a lot is Norway. My work with Richard has been featured in the two top spiritual magazines there. Medium and Magic.

Back in 2005 I was asked to work at a big show in Oslo. There I was to do readings and demonstrations of Trance Mediumship. The show was a big glitzy event with many stalls selling beautiful New Age paraphernalia. There were Healers and Mediums from all kinds of belief systems, Shamanic, Angelic, all sorts.

Quite a few Norwegian people speak some English, but I had my translator with me just in case. I had done a few readings and they had gone well. Then a lady came and sat down, and the links began to build. Her Grandmother came in and passed on lots of evidence such as memories and advice for my client's life choices. The reading was a good one with lots of validation.

Then the energy started to shift. Now through my work I've experienced a lot of weird and wonderful things. I'm not often stumped or phased. I could see my clients Grandmother standing beside her, shining like a pale hologram, but another energy was building next to her. It started like a brown ball of energy gently pulsing. Then it started to grow, becoming taller and more oval in shape.

The shape was now a lot taller and bigger than the Grandmother Spirit. I must have looked shocked because my translator asked if I was okay. Then the shape began to take form. It had hair, a LOT of hair, brown, thick and long. Then a nose started to appear, a BIG bulbous nose. It blinked at me, small shiny dark eyes, like obsidian. It was a troll.
I could hear my Invisible Friend laughing. "Well tell her then" he chuckled.

Still thinking that I finally must have lost the plot I say to my client. "Erm, you might think I'm crazy, but was your grandmother friends with a Troll?" The lady beamed. "Yes, Grandma lived in a little log cabin out in the woods, She always put food and drink out for the Trolls"

Well in this line of work you really do learn something new every day.

Trolls are as real as all other Nature Spirits.
At that show I met several spirit Trolls over that weekend – and up to this day whenever I'm working in Norway.

G is for Ghastly Apparitions;

We've all seen horror films where twisted ghosts with ghastly faces, rattle chains and moan loudly. Well thankfully spooks that look like that are rare, I say rare though because they actually do exist. I'll give you an example and then will add an explanation for why some looks so strange.

I get asked to do all sorts of very strange things in my work. (No really).

One day a while back I received a phone call about an antique Ouija board. I can't remember how the caller said that they had come by it, but they were convinced that it was acting as a gateway. As a result, they were getting a lot of unwelcome ghostly visitors in the early hours of the morning. They wanted to get rid of the board, but didn't know how to go about it, so they called me.

I drove over. I remember it was out by the Cheese Wring at Minions. If you've never been there, you really need to put on some hiking boots and go exploring. It's a beautiful wild moorland with small, twisted trees, ancient stone circles and all in the shadows of a stunning Tor called The Hurlers.

I arrive at the small Cornish cottage at the edge of the moors and was invited in by a lovely lady called Beth. She nervously uncovered the board. It was very old.

Made of slate with carved letters and edged with incised roses. It was a beautiful thing. It did have an energy though, which doesn't come as a surprise.

I thanked Beth and headed off. You can't help but feel a little odd as you drive along the winding and remote Cornish lanes with such an object beside you on the passenger seat. What things has it seen? What spirits has it channelled?

By the time I got home it was getting late. So, after fixing myself some supper and replying to my emails I head up to bed, taking the board with me and stood it in the corner of the room.

No sooner had I started to get drowsy, I feel an energy shift. Although my strongest ability as a medium is hearing, sometimes I see quite clearly too.

A whooshing energy started to build. It is growing from the centre of the board. Twisting and rising it makes its way to the ceiling. It's circling round and round at quite a pace. It starts to take form and manifests into the Spirit is a beautiful Indian woman. She is coloured all in sepia, like an old photograph. She's wearing a sari and has a bindi on her forehead. She has a nose piercing with a chain that attaches to a headpiece that she is wearing.

I watch her for a while as she flies around and around the ceiling, swooping and rising. the air is filled with the scent of sandalwood. Slowly she fades away. Then the energy changes bringing a very different vibe,

I sit up, and there next to my bookshelf is a figure beginning to manifest. He is dressed like a cavalier. High riding boots, red velvet trousers and matching jacket. Shiny brass buttons. Long dark curly hair – and the head of a pig (WTF?)

Now this creature's energy doesn't feel nice. It's dark and tainted. He looks at me with his beady eyes. He wrinkles his snout and I hear a squealing grunt.

I'm feeling unsettled to say the least. I do that thing that I do. I galvanise my energy field and lock it into my centre, then I tell him." I have NO idea what you think you're doing here, but I'm not interested, and you need to leave" -

For a minuet nothing happens. He stands there, looking at me, his toxic energy filling the room. His faintly putrid odour started to make my eyes sting.

I stick to my guns and stay focused but neutral. “There is nothing for you here, you need to go.” Then slowly after a while he fades away. After that I get up and smudge my room. “No wonder I’m a flipping insomniac I grumble”

The next morning I’m woken up by my invisible friend Richard coming in.

He has a beastly sense of humour for a spook. “I hear you had company last night” he chuckled. “Yes, I did, and thanks for coming to help me sort it out” I gripe. “And what’s with the guy with the pigs head anyway?” It’s clear from Richards buzzing energy feels that he’s amused by the whole thing. I often ask him for explanations when paranormal things happen, and he has such a matter-of-fact way of answering, as if all those crazy things are perfectly normal.

“Oh yeah right” he replies. “Yeah, it’s funny when that stuff happens. It’s all about how people have lived their lives on earth. What you do when you’re reincarnated, your thoughts and actions all affect the way that you look when you spirit leaves your body. Most people live good lives. They care for each other. They work hard and do good deeds. So when they leave their body and are in their spirit form that are all shiny and new. Perfect and beautiful manifestations of themselves. But not everyone.

If, however, someone has been sneaky and thought only of themselves, or if they’ve been dishonest then when they are in their spirit form, they might have a snake-ish or rat-ish appearance. If they were always poking their nose into other people’s affairs and gossiping, they might have a massive nose and big flabby lips like a proboscis monkey. And if they’ve been gluttonous then they may well appear like your pig man” Thanks for that Rich.

That makes perfect sense though. We are the energy that we’ve acquired

Through our thoughts and actions on the earth.

That makes me wonder what some of our world leaders will look like after their passing.

So what happened to the board? It was a beautiful thing but was clearly a gateway. Richard told me to take it to a nearby Holy Well and wash it in the water. Then I was to wrap it in a white silk scarf and bury it in the woods.

It seemed a great pity, but I couldn't risk it falling into the wrong hands again. It was made of stone, so it was only right that it be returned to the earth.

H is for Headless Horseman

My work with the paranormal takes me to many far-flung places throughout the UK and abroad, but right from the start at the beginning of the millennium our work led us to Wales.
On one such occasion I was heading up to North Wales with my best buddy David. Although the Welsh countryside is stunning it had been a long drive up from Cornwall, so we started looking for somewhere to stay.

Now to this day I can't remember the location of the Inn that this story is about. I have racked my brains because I would like to go there again, but no luck.
After a long day in the hot summer sun we stumbled upon a little village with a pub called The Royal Oak. We noticed that it had a B&B sign in the window and that was good enough for us.

We went in and booked our room. The pub was owned by a pleasant lady and her teenage daughter. Their names were Jane and Marie-ann.
The Royal Oak was very old with whitewashed walls and heavy oak beamed ceilings. The stairs up to our room were narrow and rickety and the bedroom floor listed so that you felt drunk when you walked on it.

After we had rested, we came down to eat. There were two bars, the lower of which looked out over a winding river over which hung a majestic willow tree. We sat down and made ourselves comfortable.

There were a few other guests that evening, each sat with drinks waiting for their meals. Jane was working in the kitchen and Marie-Ann was serving. Now I know that she was young, but something weird was going on. When she was working in the top bar there was no problem, but whenever she came into our room, she was making all sorts of mistakes. Giving guests the wrong meals. Dropping cutlery. Knocking over water and tripping up over her own feet. Guests teased her that she had been having a sly nip of mead, which of course she denied. It was weird.

Then I started to feel woozy. We had driven over 300 miles so I thought that I was probably tired. We decided to leave everyone to it and try to get some much-needed sleep.

The next morning, we went down to our table. The smell of bacon and eggs was wonderful and the breakfast buffet was full of local fruit, homemade hot bread rolls and tempting cereals.

Things were still the same in the downstairs bar though. Marie-Ann was still getting confused over orders and making mistakes. I felt like someone was distracting her. Something paranormal had to be going on.

I started to feel dizzy again, and I noticed that the cutlery on our table started to vibrate and rattle as if there was a mini earthquake.

Then I saw him. Over by the bar, a figure slowly started to materialise. I got the impression that he was a messenger of some kind. He was dressed in clothes from long ago, riding breeches. High leather boots with big brass buckles. A leather satchel over his shoulder. He was very good looking too. Blond hair and pale blue eyes. He smiled at me. "I knew you could see me" He grinned "You must do something for me. I'm in love with the barmaid's daughter. We met when I was on the earth in another lifetime. We were going to be married, but one morning, as I was leaving to carry a message to the King's troops, I was set upon by vagabonds and they cut my throat. You must tell them about me please" The cutlery was still rattling, and other guests were beginning to give me funny looks. I had to do something, so I took a deep breath and explained to the other guests that I was a medium and that the Royal Oak was haunted. Some nodded, others looked agog and quickly left.

Later, as we were about to leave, I asked the landlady if we could have a word. "Did you guys know that you have a ghost? This might sound weird, but he has a thing about Marie-Ann. He thinks that they were together in another life. He's a bit obsessed"

Jane told us that it all made total sense. She had thought something like that must be happening. "It's funny that you should say that" she explained. "Because when we said that we were going to buy the place locals tried to warn us off because apparently the pub is haunted by a headless horseman"

Immediately the ghostly horseman's energy went crazy, so much so that a picture that was hanging on the wall came flying off and hit the floor with a crash.

The messenger was horrified that the love of his life might think that he was haunting without his head. What chance would he have with her then if she imagined him bloody and decapitated?

"Oh, no, no" He shrieked "I'm not headless, they only cut my throat"

Bless him, he didn't want such grizzly information to spoil his chance of romance.

So we said our goodbyes and headed off on our journey. I really wish I could remember where the Royal Oak was. I'd love to go there again and see how they're all getting on. Never mind.

I is for Incubus;

Now if you Google this word most explanations that you will find go like this "Demonic entities who seduce women in their sleep." The Church likes to put a lot of spiritual phenomena down to demons. More-so if it has an element of sexuality in it. (Anything of pleasure is a sin - apparently).

Having been in this work for many moons, however, has shown me that when you have met very many people telling you the same story, without having any knowledge of each other, then you must be at least open minded.

Many objective accounts of the same thing indicate that there might at least be something in it.

Over the years, there have been occasions when, after running a workshop or some other event, a student will come up to me and say, "Can I have a word with you please?" "Yeah sure, what is it?" - "Erm no, not here, can we talk outside" and here we go again. If I had a quid for every time I'd heard the start of that conversation, I'd be able to afford a decent car by now.

The bottom line is that spirit people can fall in love, and spirit people who have passed and left a partner behind, still feel the same as they ever did on the earth. Love conquers all, including death. It really does.

Now I don't have any stories to tell about steamy liaisons between the living and the dead. Well, I do, but they are of such an intimate and private nature that it would be wrong of me to share them. However, because SO many people have confided in me, and they always imagine that I'll think they're crazy it seemed right to tackle this subject in this book. Love affairs between worlds are not at all uncommon. Really.

It's like Sam says to Molly just before he goes into the light in the film *Ghost*. *"It's amazing Molly, the love you feel, you take it with you"* - and it seems they do.

I know of so many people who have said that their partner, who had recently passed, came back for a last cwtch (Welsh word for a cuddle). I get asked all the time if that's okay, if it's wrong? It's not.

I know of one lady whose husband was serving in Afghanistan. (I have her permission to share this story)

So, he had been away for a long time, and she was really missing him. On this particular night she was feeling his absence more than ever. Miserably she climbed into bed and after a while her head became fuzzy, and she started to doze off. She told me that she started to dream. At least she thought it was a dream.

The bedroom door started to open a little, the hall light dimly illuminated the room, and there he was. Her husband was in the doorway smiling at her. Still in his army uniform. He stepped inside and started to peel his clothes off like a stripper-gram (She said.) He had always worked out and as he undressed the glinting moonlight highlighted his toned body.

He climbed into bed with her and gave her the biggest hug. Then they did what grown-ups do. She fell asleep in his arms.

The next morning, when she woke up, he wasn't there. She supposed that he was in the shower or was downstairs making coffee. Excitedly she slipped on her dressing gown and rushed downstairs, but he wasn't there. Neither was his kit bag.

She couldn't work it out, where had he gone?

Then came a knock on the door. A man and woman dressed in military uniforms were outside. Her heart sank. They had come to tell her that her husband had been killed while on duty the night before, and accounting for the time difference it happened just before he appeared in her bedroom.

The soldier had come home to say goodbye and have a last moment of intimacy before going into the light. It hadn't been a dream.

Although devastated by the news, at least they had had one last moment together - until they meet again in the Spirit World.

I have heard many personal accounts like that. So, there we are. Love is love. It really is.

J for John Harris;

John Harris was a famous Cornish Poet born on October 14th, 1820, and died on Jan 7th, 1884. His grave is in the cemetery of Treslothan Church.

I first heard about the poet when I attended a talk at the church with my son. We had been drawn to the area having found the village by chance. Right away we agreed that the whole place felt very active and we decided to drop in whenever we could to tune in to the resident ghosts and to research history.

It's quite difficult to tell this story as Treslothan and the surrounding area are pretty much the most dramatically haunted locations that I have ever encountered and there is a long chapter about that later in this book.

However, getting to know Mr Harris could have only been a good thing as in a following chapter he is a very big part of a spookily dramatic evening of paranormal activity.

Treslothan is almost otherworldly. When you drive out from the old mining town of Camborne all the buildings are as you would expect. On leaving the town there are rows of terraces that used to be dwellings for miners. As you drive further out the buildings become white walled Cornish cottages and farmlands. A little further out and things start to change. The road to Treslothan becomes narrow and is shadowed on both sides with thick woodlands. Branches intertwine overhead to make a canopy of thick leaves;

you feel the energy start to change dramatically. You are driving through a tunnel constructed by nature and there is an uneasy feeling.

Turning right, down towards the church is like stepping into another reality. So different from the traditional look of Cornwall. There are very few houses, but those that are there are large and very gothic in appearance. The church is very much the same. A large sepulchre stands ominously in the corner of the graveyard.

A little to the left is the gravestone of John Harris. Right from the start Joe and I felt very drawn to it. There were some synchronicities too. John Harris had been a Libra like me. Tragically, he had lost two children. His son Alfred who died at the age of 32, passed away on the same day and month as Joe's birthday (January 20th) and his daughter who died at six years old was called Lucrecia which is Joe's wife's middle name. So, whenever we called in on Treslothan church, we always took a moment to stop at the poet's grave.

Then we had an idea. It was to be his birthday soon, and as we felt a connection of sorts, we thought it might be nice to maybe go and read some of his poems at his graveside on his special day.

When we arrived, we greeted Mr Harris, lit some incense and wished him a happy birthday. Then Joe started to read aloud. The poem was called Falmouth Fire. (We were also using a K2 to see if there was any paranormal activity).

At first things were still but then all at once the energy started to change. The K2 was going crazy, lights flashing back and forth across the whole spectrum as the air filled with a buzzing vibration. We could feel him so clearly, it nearly took our breath away. It was as if an electric current was running right through our bodies. He was clearly so happy that we had taken the time to read his poems. What an amazing experience.

Since that day we have often stopped and talked to the Cornish Poet, and nearly always have had a response either using the K2 or clairvoyantly.
We feel now that we are friends, and on many occasions, he has given us insights and on one occasion, he delivered a very stark warning.

Joe and I decided to run an extra invest on Halloween. (Probably not our smartest move). We had arrived at Treslothan earlier than intended, so thought we'd have a quick look around and leave some offerings (Food for the wildlife etc), Then we would come back later with our paranormal equipment.

Joe had the family dog with him. Opal is a bouncy and enthusiastic King Charles Spaniel, tan and white with super-soft fluffy fur. A little princess.
While I walked her around the cemetery Joe fired up his spirit box and started to tune it in.
It wasn't long before a deep voice that we recognise as John Harris boomed out of the device. "It's coming." Joe was a bit taken aback but thought maybe he had misheard. He carried on wandering amongst the gravestones. Once again, the voice warned "It's coming." This time we both felt a bit unsettled. What was coming? Whatever it was, It was too early for a full invest, so we decided to nip to our local pub for a quick pint while we waited for twilight to draw in.

We discussed the warning while we drank our beers. Opal was bouncy and enthusiastic as ever and we wondered if maybe we should have left her at home. It's not ideal to have a yappy pup around when you're trying to connect to paranormal energies.

At last darkness fell and we headed back to complete our evening. As we drove up the lane towards Treslothan Opal jumped about enthusiastically. Hoping to get another walk, but as we arrived outside the cemetery gates, she shrank back and became quiet. The change in her demeanour was really noticeable.

It was only a moment before we understood why she was suddenly clearly very frightened.

As we got out of the car and stepped into the darkness, we were immediately hit by a wall of oppressive energy that felt like a punch in the gut. Then standing in the shadows of the trees the most ungodly sound burst from the woodland behind the church. It's hard to adequately describe, but it was something between a bark and a strangulated howl. It reminded me of the lycanthrope in American Werewolf in London. Then we remembered John Harris's warning "It's coming."

That was enough for us, we jumped back in the car and left. Poor little Opal was curled right up into a ball on Joe's lap. It was so unlike her usual behaviour, Poor little thing, she was really scared.
Joe called me later to say that it took quite a time for her to get back to her normal bouncy self. He had to give her spiritual healing with tourmaline before she settled.

Our friend John Harris definitely saved us from a close encounter on Halloween. So much for trick or treat.

K is for Kennal Vale;

Cornwall is full of weird and wonderful places, with a rich history of Pirates and Smugglers. It also has a LOT of haunted places.

One such place is Kennal Vale. Nestled in a valley in-between Falmouth and Redruth in Cornwall this picturesque woodland shelters echoes of an industrial past as a gunpowder works. As you can imagine working with explosives back in the day was a dangerous job, and the inevitable catastrophes led to many deaths and there-for the presence of ghosts and spirits

.

These days nature has reclaimed the works and millwheels, and a woodland has grown around the derelict buildings that have been swallowed by trees, ivy and moss. It's an enchanting and beautiful place, all coloured in emerald, green.

Waterfalls, streams and mill pools all add an otherworldly atmosphere to this beautiful place.

So, this is the setting for my next story. You would be forgiven for expecting us to encounter the ghost of an ill-fated worker, But no. We were to meet an entirely different energy.

As well as being a Paranormal Investigator, my son Joe is a musician and songwriter. At this time, he was working on a project for me. It was to be a meditation album which helped to induce an altered state, which would be useful for connecting to spirit to work in Trance. The album was to be called Dive, so for the cover we needed a picture of ripples spreading out over the surface of a pond. We know that Kennel Vale had mill ponds, so we decided that it would be a good place to go to capture the right sort of image.

With us was Leona Coombe. She was working with Joe on the project and was a keyboard player. She was also a practicing witch.

We made our way along the winding path deep into the woods and came upon a perfect mill pool edged with rocks and moss. It was a magical place, more so than we realised. Joe and Leona wandered around looking for the best position to take the shot and then set up the camera. I set off on a mission to find the perfect rock to throw into the pool. It needed to be fairly substantial so that when it hit the water the ripples would be very clear to see.

After a bit of searching, I found one. It was triangular and made of granite, with little flecks of quartz glittering on the surface. I bent down and picked it up and walked to the edge of the pond, ready to launch. "Let me know when you're ready to take the shot and I'll throw the rock" - I waited for my instructions. I was poised to go, when I clearly heard a shrill voice crying "Oh no no, please don't throw me into that pond. I'll never be able to get out, I'll be stuck there forever"

I stopped and froze, staring at the rock like an idiot.
"What ARE you doing?" asked the two. "You're going to think I've lost the plot" I replied - "But I just heard a voice begging me not to throw the rock into the pond" - Joe looked at me agog, but Leona, being a witch, was much wiser. "It must be a nature spirit" she explained. "The rock must be its home. We must put it back somewhere safe and leave it alone"

Leona took the rock and put it safe amongst the moss. Then she left a little piece of jam sandwich for the fairy and apologised for us frightening it. She then asked the fairy if she could take a photo.
Then we carried on with our mission and managed to collect some images without upsetting any more sprites.

When we got home and put the images on our laptop to see if we had a picture for the album cover, we came across the image of the rock. Perched on top of it we could see very faintly, a little corn coloured figure with yellow eyes and spiky green hair. It was leaning forward, looking straight into the camera. We had captured a fairy on film.

L is for Lost Souls;

Usually when someone passes over, they are met by loved ones, Guides and pets who have gone before them. However, occasionally, if someone passes over in trauma, or feel they have unfinished business, then they may be oblivious to the spirits of the people who come to meet them and take themselves off to complete whatever it is that they feel they need to do.

With suicides for example. Richard has always told me that some of them will go off and seek understanding from someone who is alive on the Earth. He says that it represents to them, a loved one or family member. Sometimes a suicide is just looking for a random person who will have sympathy and compassion towards them. Someone non-judgemental to let them know that they understood the spirit's need to let go of life and to (in a way) give them permission to go into the light.

For five years, I worked as part of a team on a very successful radio show called Haunted Cornwall FM. On one particular show we were talking about the difference in energies between dark spirits and lost souls. Some "mediums" seem not to be able to do that and treat the two the same which is very bad if a spirit needs help. Bellowing incantations in a haze of sage is not beneficial to someone who just needs a hug.

So I finished the show and drove home. After replying to messages from listeners of the show I went to bed. No sooner had I done so than the energy in the room started to change. At first the temperature in the room started to drop. Then I could hear a very faint humming. It was a female voice, tuneful, but forlorn. Then I saw her.

Manifesting from the corner of the room the spirit of a young girl started to appear. As she drifted towards me she became easier to see. She was painfully thin, waif-like. She was dressed in a white linen nighty, her red hair flowing over her narrow shoulders. Her skin was milky white with freckles, and her eyes were large, round and watery green.

The energy was intense now, and very unsettling. She was still humming as she floated right up to my face, she made deep eye contact with me. (At this point I do remember uttering an expletive "Oh F*ck"), so I galvanised myself and asked her what she wanted and was she okay. No reply.

What happened next, I can remember as clearly as the moment it happened. With one bony hand she grasped her lower jaw, and started to pull it down, further and further. Opening her mouth wide like a python swallowing large prey. Then with her other hand, she wound her long red hair around her fingers and with a quick, jabbing motion started to jam it down her throat, retching as she did.
By now I was frozen with fear. My mind raced to think of how I could defuse this escalating situation. All I could see was her green eyes, gaping mouth and tumbling red hair. As my head spun from her energy, I realised that I had begun to cough, and to my horror I could feel her thick hair winding its way into my mouth and creeping towards my throat like living tendrils, rough and wiry. Then suddenly an understanding hit me.

She wasn't there to do me harm, she was desperate for compassion and understanding. Images of her flashed through my mind. I realised in that moment, that her earthly life had been brutal and bleak, so much so that she had committed suicide by choking herself on her long red hair. My heart chakra filled with empathy "Oh you poor, poor thing," I stuttered, and in that instance, she was gone.

Bless her, I shall never forget the girl with the red hair. She was a lost soul just looking for someone to set her free. After possibly years of wandering and being unhappy, she could go into the light. I felt as if she had been in a Victorian asylum and had been miserable there. Of course, I can never know for sure what had happened to her in her earthly life, but that thought came into my mind as she let go. At least now I knew that she was free.

M is for Manifestation;

Physical Mediumship is a very rare thing. Most mediums receive messages from Spirit telepathically. Some see spirits like pale holograms or see images of them in their head using their 3rd eye. Very few ever get to experience a spirit transfiguring completely so that they are solid and touchable. I am one of the few who have been lucky enough to have that experience. I will never forget it.

Back when Richard first came to me in February 2000, he was still very raw from his passing. He needed closure on a number of things to do with his past, and in September 2000, he asked me if I would go with him back to the Welsh valleys where he had grown up. I agreed.

We set off and although I had never been to Wales before I was able to find all the places that he needed to visit, without using a map. As I got to a junction, in my head I would hear him say "Turn left, down there, see that cottage" etc. The whole journey was filled with amazing experiences, but as I said at the start of this book, we would be here forever if I wrote about them all. So, with the visit over I drove home.

That evening, he came to me. He said, "I want to show you something special tonight, so keep a clear head" (I sometimes like a glass of wine in the evening to relax, but tonight that was not allowed).

Tired after a long weekend I had a shower and climbed into bed. Now I think I have already explained that I'm chronic insomniac. This was useful on this occasion though because unbeknown to me, this was to be a long night.

After some time, I felt Richard's energy. It felt mischievous and excited. He told me that I must relax and to focus on sending him positive vibes. Slowly over several hours the frequency in the room started to change. The air was filled with static electricity that popped and buzzed.

I kept getting a little electric shock and started to feel a bit uneasy. Then I heard him laugh "Oh you're scared" he teased. "No, I'm not" I responded. "Yes, you are" He laughed again "You need to keep your eyes open for this bit" he explained.

I opened my eyes and by the side of the bed was a pillar of sparkling light. It was white with flecks of gold and spun like a whirlwind. As I gazed at it my head was filled with roaring noises. There were sounds like the ripping of fabric, then a thundering whooshing sound like a train rushing through a tunnel, then the sounds changed to a high-pitched ringing and whining in my ears and as it did the pillar of energy lifted until it was hanging just above my bed. It was as if time stood still.

Slowly the spinning stopped, and the light began morphing into a figure. It was Richard, clear as day. I don't know how long the moment lasted. I told myself to take in every feature of his face. I had, had issues with who he was right from day one. Maybe this was why he worked so hard to manifest, so that I had seen him with my own eyes and would doubt no more.

I could see him, solid from the waist up. He was shining like a moonstone, his eyes were clear like mirrors. The energy was sublime, I felt intoxicated as if I had taken opium. Then, all at once an amazing thing happened, he dropped down from above and grabbed hold of me and hugged me tightly. He felt solid but cold as if he had come in from the garden on a winter's night. I could feel his hair on my cheek, "Thank you" he whispered, and then he was gone, and my room returned to normal.

I supposed the thank you was for going with him to say goodbye to the place where he has grown up. I also think it was because I had always promised to try my very hardest to get his message home that he was okay. Whatever the reason, I know that he had to work very hard to give me that experience. And I will treasure that moment forever.

N is for Nun;

This story goes way back to when I was a very young girl, around five years old. My childhood was a turbulent one and my mother and father had a very fractured relationship. There were often explosive arguments, and my father could sometimes be violent. On one occasion this was the case. Things had been particularly bad and so my mother had packed a few things and had driven us down to my aunt's caravan park in Herne Bay in Kent, to give Dad time to cool off. It was quite late when we arrived. We were both tired and shell shocked by what had happened earlier, so Mum made up the beds and we settled down for the night.

Now this was back in the day, caravans weren't like the plush mobile homes of today. This one was quite small with a narrow seating area at the far end, which twinned as single beds. This is where we were to sleep. Mother drifted off quite quickly, but me, still being upset by the events of the day, was wide awake.

In the 60's caravans had no electricity, so lights and cookers were powered by gas. Mum had left the gas lights on dimly to give some light to the otherwise, pitch-black room.

As I lay in bed I started to see, at the far end of the caravan, a little orb of light beginning to grow. I watched it with fascination. It grew bigger and as it did it started to drift towards me and to take the shape of a young girl. As the figure became clearer, I could see that it was a little novice Nun holding a rosary.

I sat up, wide eyed and watched as the little figure glided above the caravan floor. Each time she passed one of the gas lamps they went "POP" and went out.
By now she was level with my bed, I was spellbound and unable to speak but her energy was lovely. As she got level with me, she turned and smiled and then she vanished through the caravan wall.
At that point I found my voice "Mum, mum I've just seen a ghost" I shrieked. Mum was awake instantly and reassured me that it must have been a dream. I knew that it wasn't.

The following night, as I slept soundly, Mum saw the same thing. We believe that the little Nun was a spirit guide or messenger, who had come to reassure us that we were being looked after. She was my first encounter with a supernatural being. She was lovely.

O is for Over-shadowing

The number one ability that Richard and I became known for. The thing that got us invitations to work all over the world was Trance mediumship.
Trance really is just a more advanced type of mediumship; it is also practiced by many different spiritual religions all over the world and especially so amongst indigenous people during festivals and ceremonies. It is also referred to as channelling, although that really is a less advanced form.

When I/we are booked for a demonstration, I always explain to our audience how it works. The easiest way to do this, I find, is to ask if anyone had seen the film, Ghost. (Most people have) Then I tell them to think of the part where Whoopi Goldberg's character has become a genuine medium, and she is sitting at the table with spirits queueing up wanting her to pass on messages to loved ones. One spirit, a larger gentleman, becomes impatient and "jumps into" the medium's body and starts to speak through her. This is what I do with Richard, although in our case it's by arrangement.

Because what we do is an advanced form of mediumship, I am often asked to run workshops so that people can attempt to connect to their Guides in this way. The aim is to be a clear channel for their Invisible Friends, to give them a voice in this world. Some duos can do it, others can't. I suppose it all depends on if this is your path.

There are varying degrees of Trance and Channelling. It's like rungs on a ladder really. At the lightest levels the medium would be very aware of what is going on and could block the information if they felt that it wasn't appropriate for the situation.

Further along the progression, the medium would be less aware of what was being said by the connected spirit and it would be much harder to stop the dialogue from continuing.

In deep Trance the medium is unaware to a large degree of what the spirit is saying, as he or she communicates in a free-flowing manner with an audience. (This is the level that I work with Richard).

Sometimes when a spirit comes in to talk through a medium it is also called overshadowing and I have an example to share of just how strong the connection can be.

On this occasion I was running a workshop in Norfolk and had a prodigy called Theresa with me. She had travelled and worked with me extensively and was a very promising medium and Channel. The group was quite large, so when it came time for them to attempt the exercise, I put Theresa in charge of a small group. As I walked around observing my student's progress, I became aware of a bit of a hoo-haa coming from her table.

When I got there, I understood why. It was hilarious. So, Teresa was preparing to give a demonstration of channelling/Trance to her table. She had explained the process, put herself into an open state and invited her Guide William in. She had not at this point closed down her awareness completely, so could still hear what was going on, she was still very present.

As William started to connect and prepared to speak to the group, he suddenly stopped and went "Urgh", contorting Teresa's face into a grimace. (She was aware that this was happening, but having stepped back she had no control over it). One of the students asked him what was wrong, William sounded horrified "Ugh, she's chewing GUM. IT'S DISGUSTING" he moaned. Trying to be helpful, one of the students offered "Here spit it out", and held out her hand. Theresa was horrified and in her mind was YELLING at William "Don't you DARE", but of course there was nothing that she could do to stop him, and with a great deal of force he spat the lump of chewing
gum into the open palm.

At that point I arrived at the table. Theresa was back and was SO embarrassed. She couldn't believe what William had just done. I had to say what a brilliant example of overshadowing it was. Even though she had been aware, William was so well connected that she couldn't prevent his actions.
When a duo work at that level, it's quite an achievement. I don't think Theresa ever forgave William for what he had done, even though it showed what a talented couple they were.

P is for Paris;

I had been interested in the Paris Catacombs for a very long time. Eventually I arranged to visit with two friends of mine, Vivian and Dave Llewellyn. Both well respected healers and mediums.

The catacombs are situated in the centre of Paris and at first you could easily mistake the building as a library or museum with its ornate architecture and classic wrought iron fencing. On the day we decided to go we were lucky that it was very quiet. Only a few other people were queuing to visit.

Going through the front door you come to a spiral staircase made of the same wrought Iron as the fence outside. Descending round and round deeper and deeper into the earth there is a dense musty smell and the further you go down, the less light there is. As you arrive at the lower chamber, the only illumination is from little upturned lights buried in the cave-like walls.

The layout of the catacombs is a series of tunnels, at the end of which is an archway inscribed with the name of a cemetery, as you go under that you find yourself in an igloo shaped, domed space filled from floor to ceiling with the bones of the dead. You can reach out and touch them, you can lift a skull and hold it. It is a very strange feeling knowing that all of these were once people who lived a life like you and me. Ashes to ashes, dust to dust.

We started to explore, wandering from chamber to chamber, then I started to feel unwell. Dave and Vivian were chatting, looking around. Neither of them was affected, but I began to feel lightheaded and started to cough. "You okay" asked the guys "Yes fine" was my answer, I wasn't.

My cough felt dry, and my lungs started to burn. It was as if I had inhaled mustard. The further I went the more unsteady I became. A strong taste of iron filled my mouth, I recognised it as blood. Whenever I coughed, the taste increased. I was starting to think that maybe I might have to ask the boys for help, but I didn't want to spoil their experience, so I held on.

Exploring ever deeper we walked on into the Ossuary (which translates from French as "Stop - This is the empire of death) Deeper now,
the catacombs at their base are more than 65 feet to the lowest chamber. A descent of 131 steps.

I am still feeling unwell. My throat is so dry, and every breath burns. The taste of blood is making me feel sick. I am just about to ask for help as we pass under another archway arriving in a huge chamber that feels like a cave. It's hard to believe that we were still in Paris.

We have arrived at the Fountain of the Samaritan a natural underground spring, and as we do I feel a rush of energy, it's not mine, not physical, but from a lady spirit drawing near. I recognised at once the symptoms that I had been feeling were not mine, they were hers. She had been showing me that she had contracted Tuberculosis and it had claimed her life.
Her body was now somewhere here in the chamber with all the others.
For a moment I could see her like a sepia photograph. She was wearing period clothes, a long dress, bonnet and shawl. She just wanted to share her experience with someone, as is quite often the case.

All that some ghosts need before they can move on into the light is a little understanding and empathy. I felt her energy leave and go into the light and I was once again back to my old self.

Q is for Queensland;

Over a five-year period, up until 2010 (When my mother became ill, and I had to stay closer to home to be there for her) I worked quite extensively around Australia. Because it's such a big country I used to fly from one booking to another, but on my last trip there I decided to take a few friends and hire a car so we could drive across the country. (Tony and Krishna were mediums and David was a healer) This was the biggest tour that I had undertaken in Australia. We were to run workshops. Do readings and demonstrations and offer healing sessions as we travelled,

I didn't know at the time, but this was to be my last visit to Australia for a many years. Australia is the most wonderful place with its golden beaches and clear blue sea, not to mention all those weird and wonderful animals and birds, but one of the things that I liked most was the smell. Hot and earthy, the aroma of the desert.

We started our work in Sydney, then went to Tasmania, then to Perth and all along the Gold and Sunshine coasts. We covered hundreds of miles and met a lot of interesting people who were all looking for their spiritual path. When our last booking was done, we decided to take our time and wander around exploring, getting the timing right to catch our plane back at Sydney airport.

One time as we were heading back, we found ourselves in a dusty old mining town. It had a dilapidated hotel. Hanging outside by one rusty chain was a sign saying “accommodation available”.

The building looked like something out of the wild west. Rickety and wooden just like in the old cowboy movies. We decided to book rooms anyway. Although two of our party weren't at all keen, we were too far away from anywhere else to look for somewhere different.

We were given the number of our room (There were no keys and no locks on the doors) so we went to settle in. What a shock we got. I thought it was hilarious. The rooms had no carpets, just rough bare boards. The beds were all shapes and sizes and looked like they had come from random auctions. The bedding although clean was all different, as if it had been bought from a jumble sale. Krishna and David were nervous and decided to stay in the room, where 'as Tony and I went downstairs to see if we could get food and a drink.

The bar staff were two young girls. They were lovely. The "locals" were all workers from the local mine, and to use a Cornish expression, they were rough as rats. Shaved heads, tattoos, missing teeth, what a bunch of characters. They were friendly though and of course they asked what we were doing there. I took a big breath, and I told them. To say they took the p*ss was an understatement. But I'm okay with that. They started to buy us drinks and as the night wore on, they became more and more drunk. (and so were we).

The old saloon had an amazing jukebox. All favourite Rock and metal tunes created a very fitting atmosphere for such a wild place. Then as Metallica boomed out *Unforgiven*, one of the barmaids asked for a reading. The other piped up that she would like one too. Tony went with one girl and I read for the other. Everything went really well and when we got back to the bar the locals asked how it had gone?

A lot of banter followed, then one particularly massive Aussie came over to me and asked if I would read for him ("Oh sh*t"). I did though.

We found a quiet corner and as soon as we sat down his loved ones from the spirit world crowded in. For such a big guy he'd obviously had a very difficult

private life and had become estranged from his children, His mother came through and reassured him, giving him advice to contact his daughter that night because she missed him too. He cried like a baby bless him.
After the reading he called his daughter, and the situation was happily resolved.
The rest of the evening was a tremendous experience as we swapped stories with the miners. The next morning when we set off on our journey home. Tony and I had massive hangovers. Them Aussies know how to party.

So we travelled on, finding random places to stay as the day became night. On the final day we found an old roadhouse. It reminded me of Bates Motel in Psycho. We booked two chalets. One for the boys and the other for Krishna and me. After eating in the diner and having a few glasses of wine we turned in for the night.

Krishna and I were in bed watching rubbish on the TV. I had taken a sleeping pill and was becoming drowsy, then in my head I heard Richard say "You need to check your ticket" - I replied, "it's okay I know what time we fly tomorrow." Again, he repeated in my head "No, really, you need to check." This time I ignored him. Then almost yelling at me he ranted "Will you check that F*cking ticket!" His voice was so loud that it actually made me jump and I yelled back "Oh all right shut up nagging me." I started to rummage around in my case. "What on earth are you doing?" Krishna asked. "He says I have to check my ticket but I know when we fly".

By now I had found our itinerary. I looked at it in disbelief. We were in the middle of nowhere and it was past midnight. We had got it wrong, and we only had six hours to reach the airport.

I went and knocked on the boy's cabin. "I have a surprise for you guys" Bleary eyed Tony joked "What do you have a spider in your plughole" - "No, actually we only have six hours to get to the airport or we're going to miss our flight" -

A very big panic ensued.

We piled into the car but having had wine and a sleeping pill I was in no state to drive. Tony had to take the wheel and had to drive through the night to get us to Sydney in time to catch our flight. What a hero.

We did arrive in time. A little worse for wear. But I was so grateful that Richard had nagged me. If he hadn't done so we would have missed our flight for sure, and it would have cost an arm and a leg to buy another to get us home. On more than one occasion he's proved to be the most invaluable spook.

R is for Richard;

Although I have told this story hundreds of times, no book I ever wrote would be complete without including my Invisible Friend Richard. Had he not come into my life and turned everything upside down. I would probably still be running my Karate clubs and caring for abused horses at my rescue centre.

There's a saying "If you want to make God laugh tell him what your plans are" That was very much the case for me. I intended to carry on teaching martial arts until I retired. There wasn't a plan B.

Right from the start of the Millennium things felt weird. I have been psychic since the age of fourteen and have always done readings. The whole "life after death" thing just made sense to me. However, I never thought that I would end up working as a professional medium, channel and teacher. That thought never crossed my mind. That was something that my other people did, weird people, mystics. Not me.

I'll never forget a conversation that I had with my blacksmith Tony Marr one frosty December morning. He always had a sarcastic edge. As he parred away at the hoof of an old chestnut mare called Magic, he laughed and joked about how some people thought the millennium was going to have "spiritual significance" - I chuckled too, little did I know what was just around the corner.

From early on in the New Year, I started having weird dreams and visions. and lots of paranormal experiences. Books would jump off shelves and fall open at pages that seemed to have insights or messages. One anthology featured a poem that appeared to be haunting me. It was The Hound of Heaven by Francis Thompson. It was everywhere, all the time and echoed in my head;

"I fled Him, down the nights and down the days; I fled Him, down the arches of the years; I fled Him, down the labyrinthine ways of my own mind; and in the mist of tears"

It was the same with music too. My car radio would suddenly turn on by itself and a song would play that seemed relevant.

I kept dreaming of a fast-flowing river. Tidal and wild and sometimes with great waves rushing out to sea. The river felt very deep and dark. The current was so strong. I had a powerful sense that someone had died there, and that I should go and put flowers into the water for them on the pagan festival of Imbolc. All of this all made no sense to me and for the most part I pushed the thoughts away.

The flowers that I kept seeing in my dreams were African violets, a deep shade of purple. So, on the morning of Feb 1st, I resolved to drive into town, get the flowers and do as I had been shown, in hope that the dreams and visions would stop. When I arrived at my local florist in Helston though, they didn't have any. So, to me that was a sign that it was all rubbish, and I should forget about the whole thing.

That though, was not going to be possible.

That night, after I went to bed, battling to sleep as usual. I felt the energy begin to change in the room. It crackled and popped and became stronger and unyielding. There was an aura, a shift. The atmosphere was tangible. I felt dizzy and disorientated. Sitting up in bed, to my amazement, I saw the Spirit of a young man standing in the corner of my room. He had dark hair, was quite thin and was wearing a black leather jacket. He stood quietly, just watching me. He looked as if he felt cold.

Now although I had been psychic for most of my life, I had never seen a spirit as clearly as that. He gave me goosebumps. Suddenly I lost my nerve and dived beneath my duvet. It was a totally primal flight or fight reaction.
I was so angry with myself. I was a martial arts instructor, I was supposed to be tough, but nevertheless I stayed hidden until he went away.

The next night he appeared again, standing quietly, but he was SO visual that I couldn't deal with it, moments later he faded away.

After that he stopped appearing and instead started talking to me. So now I'm going round "hearing voices". I thought that maybe I was ill.
Psychotic episodes though, as far as I know, don't provide you with checkable facts. Over a two-week period, I was clairaudiently bombarded with historical and geographical information. There was no Google back then, so I would have to go to the library to check the information - it was always correct. He also liked to tell me over and over again, what time it was. It's 3am. It's 6.45. It's midnight. It was always right. Then he would say "If I can tell you the time and you didn't see the clock, then I have to be real, don't I?" If I lost something he would immediately tell me where it was.
He was never wrong. I tried to rationalise what was happening, I tried to ignore it. I hoped it would go away. It didn't.

A couple of weeks later I was sitting in my front room playing my guitar. It was February and very cold. I began to notice the temperature drop, breathing out my breath became steam. Then In my head I heard a soft, lilting, male voice lamenting "There was no time to say goodbye, I didn't say goodbye"

This was getting crazy. "What the hell is going on" I asked myself. Then without warning there was a shift. A realisation. "Oh my God, I have someone with me," and then with total clarity and lucidity I heard his name "Richard"

S is for SLS:

Although I have been naturally mediumistic since my early teens, I have recently also become more interested in the use of Paranormal paraphernalia. Over the last decade there have been massive advancements in gadgets of all sorts, some of which seem to perform well and seem to give a reasonable standard of accuracy. I guess that this shouldn't be too much of a surprise though because supernatural beings have always been able to use electronic devices to draw attention to themselves.

Poltergeists or just regular spirits who are feeling a lot of emotion find it pretty easy to make lights flicker, flatten batteries on phones and cameras or to turn your TV on and off, and more recently that people have heard their Alexa answering questions in the dead of night. Spooks love to play with stuff like that.
So it's not a surprise that some paranormal equipment does seem to channel spirit communications very well.

My favourite is a very simple item that most people can easily afford. It's called K2 meter. It's been long recognised that spirits and ghosts emit an electromagnetic field and K2s can pick up on that. When your K2 is on, as you wander around an old building or the likes, you will see that the lights activate when a spirit is near. If you are clairsentient, you'll find that around the time you start to sense a presence, the light will come on, on your device to confirm that. But that's not all that a K2 can be used for. They are really a very useful tool for communication.

Once you have established a connection with a Spirit being, you can ask it if it would like to talk to you using the device to indicate yes or no. The spirit will probably confirm its interest by lighting up your device vigorously. So, then you ask a simple question as follows, for example. "If you are a man can you light up the device, please" - if it lights up, you're talking to a male, if not, it's a female. You can build on this, asking more questions so that the spirit can share information about itself with you. Many energies are more than happy to do that.

There are very many gadgets, but I won't talk too much about that. You can research for yourself online. Instead, I'll share a story about when I used a different gadget. An SLS device.

An SLS camera is used by ghost hunters to detect human shaped energies that are not visible to the human eye. Working in a similar way to a security camera they latch on to movement even in the darkest surroundings. Then, so that the investigator can see where the spirit is, the camera creates a stick image to highlight that something has been found. It was an SLS camera that I was using in this next story.

I believe that it's important for everyone to have a passion. Although mediumship and the paranormal are an important part of my life, my 2nd love is Mountain Biking and Cycling. There's nothing I love more than wandering around the trails and discovering new places.

One of my best riding buddies is called Jane. She's interested in the paranormal too. Whenever we're out in a different area, we're always looking for old, ruined buildings or churchyards. Always trying to find really old gravestones. Jane is very interested in local history and is quite knowledgeable, often, she'll be reading a memorial, wondering about the fate of the person who is buried there, when she'll go all goose-bumpy. (Spirits often come to see who's reading their stone).

Anyway, I had recently got an SLS device and had taken it out on a ride with us. It was the first time that I had tried it out. This was daytime too. Not late at night. As we cycled along a bumpy track, we came upon a cemetery that we hadn't seen before. We dismounted and started to wander around, reading the inscriptions and admiring the stone masonry.

I turned on the SLS. This was a very large area, with very many memorials. The SLS was flickering but not picking up much. Then, suddenly, there was the shape of a person, clearly showing up through the device screen.

The stick man was hovering above one of the stones. We wandered over. The closer we got, the more it started hopping around. Jane and I both started to get goose bumps. We walked over and read the name, "Steven Carson" - the inscription said "Irreplaceable Dad" - looking through the view finder we could see the shape almost dancing now and we could both feel his energy buzzing. This spirit was really happy.
Then Jane read out the lettering inscribed on his memorial. It was then that we realised that today would have been his birthday. No wonder there were so many flowers laid by his headstone and no wonder he was so full of energy. It was his special day.

We stayed and chatted to Steven for a while. He was such a cheerful energy and seemed to really enjoy our interaction with him. Before we left, we made sure to wish him a Happy Birthday. It was clear that he was celebrating.

Richard has told me many times that in the Spirit World all spiritual festivals are celebrated, as well as birthdays and transition days. It seems that over there they will use any excuse for a party.

Later, I edited the footage that we captured and put it on YouTube. The SLS worked so well on that occasion.

T is for Tales of Treslothan

This section is a collaboration between my son Joe and myself. We have both run extensive investigations in and around this area and have had many shared paranormal experiences.

Treslothan is often described as a model Gothic village and dates back to the 1840s but there is evidence of much earlier settlements. I first came upon Treslothan while out cycling, it was like I had ridden through a portal into another time. The architecture reminded me of Bram Stoker's Dracula film. The tall granite buildings with their steeply pitched roofs, front facing gables and carved pillars could easily spark imaginings of dark secrets.

I knew that my son Joe would want to visit. He's always been a fan of all things Gothic. So, the next time I went to Treslothan was with Joe and we spent the afternoon exploring the church, graveyard and mausoleum. I remember at the time how he said that Treslothan reminded him of some of the poems by Edgar Allan Poe and we both agreed that the setting had a very unique energy and slightly unsettling atmosphere.

The Mausoleum was particularly striking. With its tall arched supporting pedestals and dark wrought iron gates. We walked along the mossy paths as they wound between the graves and rhododendron trees, scrutinizing the

granite and slate headstones. The craftsmanship in their scrolling chiselled letters, cut by the hand of skilled masons, were an artform in itself. . The stones were very old, mostly early 18th century. Deeply engraved letters were weathered by the rain, other monuments were sinking into the earth and leaning at angles, covered by ivy and other sprawling climbing plants.
As we were leaving, we saw on the parish notice board that there was to be a talk soon with a local historian. We thought that it would be a good idea to attend and that was what we did.

Considering that Treslothan is a fair distance off the beaten track a surprisingly large number of people came along for the talk.
As David Thomas (The Historian) led the group around, talking about the architecture and sharing tales of old, he suddenly changed track and asked if anyone felt that Treslothan was a spiritual place. Multiple hands were raised. He then went on to recount tales from several local people who have experienced ghostly sightings, even adding that he himself had once looked over his shoulder only to see that spectre of Lady Tryphena, floating in the air and watching him as he sat taking notes about the headstones. He was such a grounded and logical man and it seemed unlikely that his experience was untrue.
Leading the group down a narrow path that ran between the woodland and an open field he paused and told us about a man, who had sworn on oath that he had been chased across the field by a spectral black dog who had emerged from Stennack woods, then he turned and lead us all back to the church for refreshments.

After the talk Joe and I agreed that we needed to look more into the supernatural side of things there, so we resolved to come back again soon and to bring our paranormal equipment with us to see if it could detect anything. There was a Full Moon due in a week, so we decided that would be a good time to start our investigations, but we could have had no idea what profound experience that was to be.

On the next Full Moon, we started our evening outside the crypt. As the mist rolled in, Joe turned on his spirit box and stood listening as it scanned through the frequencies. It wasn't long before we could hear an eerie female voice. We sensed that it was Lady Tryphena although we couldn't quite catch what she was saying. Next, we tried the church door, but being late the church was now locked, so we turned our attention to the woods and made our way down the path that ran alongside the field.

Wandering along in the twilight we could feel the atmosphere changing and there was an eerie sensation which made us both feel unsettled. A little further down the path I started to film Joe to make a video for YouTube. Joe was chatting into the camera explaining about the sightings of a black dog when suddenly, from all directions came an explosion of barking and howling as if every hound in surrounding farms and villages had been triggered by an unseen force. This could have been a coincidence, but judging by the uncanny atmosphere we knew that there was more to it than that.

Although we were pretty shaken by the experience, we continued down the trail towards Stennack woods. Climbing over a granite stile we found ourselves in an opening in the woods in the middle of a crossroads of footpaths. A heavy canopy of tree's cast dark shadows, while the upper branches intertwined like skeletal fingers.

We turned on our head torches and at once we could feel a heavy and foreboding presence building. It seemed to come from one of the footpaths that lead deep into the woods. The energy intensified, hitting both of us at once straight in the solar plexus. What happened next is difficult to do justice to. Suddenly a number of things happened in quick succession. Firstly, Joe went to take a picture with his phone, and I switched on my GoPro. We both pointed our devices in the direction of the pitch-dark trail ahead of us and then, all at once everything took a turn for the worse. Joe's phone and my camera froze, capturing the same image. It resembled a deep, black cave like a portal in the centre of the crossroads. Neither of us could switch off our devices and my GoPro began to overheat. I started to panic in case my camera's battery caught fire. I fumbled to pull it out and managed to dislodge it before it became too hot to hold. Joe put his hand in his pocket to fire up his spirit box to try to capture any voices only to receive a sharp electric shock as it shorted out and crashed. You hear all the time how entities can affect paranormal devices, but this was another level, whatever was out in the woods, didn't want us capturing or recording anything.

Waves of darkness rumbled through the trees and then a sharp "SNAP"; as a nearby branch broke. Something was moving very quickly towards us. It was at that point that we realised how unprepared we were for such an unearthly encounter and made a very swift exit. As we hurried back up the path by the field it seemed to be longer than before and the echoes of barking dogs and other eerie sounds didn't help one bit.
That was to be the first of many happenings that were to utterly convince us that the Black Dog of Stennack woods was a very real phenomenon, and something that we should find time to investigate more fully. I have worked for decades as a medium and paranormal investigator, but in all that time, I have never found a more haunted place. There are so many different levels of activity. It was on that evening that Joe and I agreed to run an investigation on every full moon from that night forward.

Although this would have been a fitting place to finish this section on, I want to talk a little more about our experiences with the black dog.
Over the last year Joe and I have visited Treslothan on every full moon and also on pagan festivals like the Summer Solstice and Halloween.
During that time, we have had powerful connections with three predominant energies there. The poet John Harris nearly always connects with either of us.

His energy is very friendly, and it feels as if he likes and appreciates our visits. Lady Tryphena also comes in frequently, particularly with Joe, and then there's the black dog.

On one occasion Lee Jones of Frome Paranormal was visiting. Joe and Lee have been good friends for many years, so Joe wanted Lee to experience the energy in and around Treslothan.

It was late in the evening and although dark, the sky was clear and full of stars. Lee and Joe were working with a Spirit box at the foot of the mausoleum when a female voice began to break through the static on the device. I stood back a little way and took out my phone to capture an image of the guys working together, however Lady Tryphena decided to put in an appearance. As I raised my phone to take the shot, an energy rose up and vanished through the top archway of the mausoleum. Whenever she has been seen it's said that she wears a long white gown, and this could clearly be seen in the photograph. We were all thrilled with the image.

It's funny how sometimes, you don't realise that you are being guided. Even though mediumship is my day job, occasionally I find myself following a series of synchronicities, only to find myself in the right place at the right time.

So one morning, quite early, returning from another venture, Joe and I decided to take my dog Meg for a walk around The Giant's Quoit. When we got there

however, the small space where two cars can normally park, had been commandeered by a badly parked 4x4. Disappointed, we decided to give Meg a quick walk at Stennack woods.

As Meg dragged me up the muddy path, I was keeping a look out for roots and rocks, but Joe was less distracted. "Bloody hell" he gasped, "Take a look at this."

It had been raining heavily for a good few days. The ground was slippery and sodden, but there on the ground were the most enormous paw prints. They were massive. A horse must have come up the same path earlier, and we noticed that in one spot there was the print of a horseshoe, with the paw print on top. Whatever left the print must be at least as big as a Dartmoor pony.

We followed the tracks and found that they started in the centre of the crossroads, exactly where the vortex opens, and then travelled along a side track into the
cemetery, right up to the Mausoleum. Another thing that struck us was that there were no boot marks in the mud. No human person had been walking with this creature.
We took some photos with our phones, but the images didn't do them justice, so I rushed into town and brought some plaster of Paris to make casts to capture the dimensions of the pads and especially the massive claws.

Later when we shared our findings, people said that maybe the footprints had been made by a big cat. (Panthers and cougars are sometimes seen around the moorlands of Cornwall) but after researching it was found that all cats retract their claws when they walk. So that was out. Really, the prints look like those of a bear or a really large wolf. I'm sure that we were guided to find the tracks that morning. The spirits of Treslothan often reward our dedication with supernatural experiences. This was another such gift, of that, I'm sure.

Over time we have had many unsettling but interesting encounters with the beast (as we sometimes call it). Here's another story.

Recently on another of our full moon invests Joe and I were making our way back through the woods, returning from the quoit. The energy was building as the vortex began to open.

As we walked up the path towards the church, I mentioned that I could feel something following us. There was a prickling sensation right behind me. When we arrived at the mausoleum, I turned on my Seer app to see if it picked up any images. I thought that maybe Lady Tryphena was with us. Suddenly we heard what sounded like something landing with two heavy thuds right in front of us, just where the woods meet the graveyard, there was a rustle of leaves, a snapping of twigs, and branches creaked as a large powerful and powerful form began to move towards us. I held my position as long as I dared but this was a big creature, and it was moving fast. It wouldn't have been a good idea to stay any longer, we both bolted back to the car and headed for home.

When I got in I checked the footage on my phone. The video was too dark to see anything much, just the silhouette of the trees bending in the moonlight. Although that was disappointing, I did manage to capture the thundering of heavy footsteps, the creaking of branches and the rustling of leaves

.

Over time we have realised that the black dog is a very real entity, and our research is ongoing. The crossroads in Stennak woods seems to be a portal between dimensions. At certain times the vortex opens, and the beast crosses over into this world. It seems, at first it is in spirit form. Its aura is very potent. As the beast heads up towards the mausoleum it takes a winding, rocky side path. As it does so it becomes more and more corporal and by the time it arrives, it has manifested completely. (Hence the footprints). I often set up a trail camera in the cemetery or at the crossroads, and we hope, at some point, to capture its image. (I'd much rather that, then to meet it face to face – but you never know.

U is for Universe;

These stories aren't about Ghosts or Spirits, but I do believe that they come in the "Paranormal" category.
Now I'm not a religious person. I don't follow any organised religion. I don't believe in a God in any sense. However, I have noticed that there does seem to be "Something up there" - I believe that the Universe is sentient.

Over the years I have heard, seen and experienced occasions when a request has been "put out there", and quite often it's as if it has been heard and responded too. But sometimes, when the wish has been granted, it is very much a double-edged sword. I'll give you two examples. One is mine, and the other is from a friend. I have her permission to tell her story.

My account takes place during the covid scamdemic.
During lockdown I found myself homeless. I had sold my tiny property but the influx of 2nd homeowners (who came flooding into Cornwall, buying up all of our cottages) pushed up house prices so I and many others could no longer afford to own a property here (Don't even get me started).
My only solution seemed to be to move away, so I started to look for somewhere in Wales (Which I have always thought of as my spiritual home).

During this time in lockdown, we were allowed to travel if we were viewing a property. I had seen a tiny flat in Mid Wales and decided to drive up to see it. I was intending to make an offer with the small amount of cash that I had left if the property was suitable.

.

I had been sofa surfing at my friend David's house, and as we were living in the same home we were allowed to travel together.
Before leaving however, I spent some time and sent my thoughts out to the Universe, "If I'm not supposed to buy this flat can you send me a sign",

The drive up from Penzance was going well, we had just started out across

Bodmin Moor. I pulled over into the layby (I can't remember what for) but as I went to rejoin the carriageway my car's engine started to roar. It got louder and louder and thick black smoke billowed out from under the bonnet. I quickly turned off the engine. The smoke still streamed out. The fuel injectors had jammed. (The RAC guy told me later that I was lucky that the car didn't burst into flames.)

I had asked the Universe to give me a sign. NOT ONE LIKE THAT!!!" I didn't want it to blow my car up. Anyway, I couldn't get to see the flat. So, my dilemma was solved. Thanks for that Universe.

On top of that, because of lockdown rules, neither the policeman nor AA guy who came out, was allowed to give us a lift. Luckily, we had our bikes with us. So, we had to cycle 45 miles back to Penzance. (There were a LOT of big hills) but hey, I guess the Universe had heard my request and had stopped me from (probably) making a big mistake.

When I got home, I posted my story on Facebook. My friend Veritee shared her story.

She and Barry had been together for years. They were one of those rare couples, for whom marriage had worked (Sorry to sound cynical).
However Barry worked away at sea, so there were long periods of time that Veritee was alone, and she missed him.
Veritee is a dog lover and artist, and her spirituality leans towards Paganism with a hint of witchy-ness.

One day, when Barry had been away for a long time Veritee got frustrated. She told me how she had ranted at the Universe saying she was tired of being alone in their big, remote, farmhouse. She yelled "I want him back, and I don't care how it happens" - A while went by and then Barry returned home, feeling unwell.

For a while they thought he was just tired. Or maybe he was run down. Working at sea is very demanding, both physically and emotionally, so being burned out wasn't unusual for someone in that work. Time went by and things were up and down, so eventually Barry went for tests. When the results came back the news wasn't good. While Barry was away, he had contracted HIV. On coming home, he had given it to Veritee. She had him home for good. But at a cost to them both.

When I asked Veritee if I could share her story, she said that she has noticed that when people make requests, or cast spells they very often get what they asked for. But often at a price.
Maybe the Universe has a twisted sense of humour? Of maybe balance is needed when fate is tweaked. Maybe it requires a quid pro quo?

So my advice is "Be careful what you wish for."

V is for visitation;

This is just a short story. It's not my own experience. It was told to me by my mother, many years ago. I was an only child. Sadly, that was not my parents' intention. My mother had Rhesus negative blood, and as a result, after having me, she has difficulties carrying another child to long term.

Years went by, with many disappointments, then one day mum found out that she was pregnant again. My parents were overjoyed. The pregnancy went
well and at the end of nine months my mother went into labour. Unfortunately, the patter on tiny feet was not to be, and my brother, who was to be called Adam, was stillborn. My mother was heartbroken, I don't think

that she ever got over the loss. On every anniversary of his birthday, she would light a candle and do something special for him.

The years rolled by, and although things were never good between them, my parents stayed together. My Father worked in the city, but also, as a hobby, owned a small antique shop in our village. He was always bringing curious objects home. We never knew what would be waiting for us when we got in.

So this morning, Dad had gone out and my Mum was upstairs changing the bed linen. She started downstairs, arms full of sheets and pillowcases, when what she saw by the front door made her drop the lot.

There in the hallway was the most beautiful statue of an angel. It looked as if it was made of rutilated quartz. It shone like moonstone and had little pink veins running right through it.

"What a beautiful thing" she thought. "How on earth did Kevin get that in here without me hearing? It must be really heavy." As she gazed at the sculpture, she noticed that the angel was holding a garland of pink rosebuds that trailed right down to the floor.

Spellbound she admired the sculpture, taking in every feature in detail, gazing at the intricate perfection of each feather of the wing. "However, could a sculptor make something so delicate?" her gaze followed up and up to see the top of the wings, but there was no top, the angel's wing-tips went straight through the ceiling. The angel was real.

As my mother stood there stunned at this realisation the most wonderful feeling flooded over her. She described it as an experience of pure love and understanding, and then, in that instance, she remembered that it was Adam's birthday, this was the first year that she had forgotten. The angel had come to remind her of that. As soon as she realised, the angel gently faded away.

Sometime after my mother died, I was at Mazy Day, (A yearly festival in Penzance). There was a fortune teller sitting at a table in the high street. I noticed that throughout the day she had no-one come for a reading.
I decided to ask her to read for me. She was really very good and gave me lots of relevant information. Then she suddenly stopped and looked thoughtful saying "Your mother is in the spirit world. You have a brother there too. His name is Adam. He says it's his turn to look after Mum now." It was so nice to hear that they were finally together.

W is for Witches:

As I have said earlier. I come from a family of mediums and witches on my mother's side. Although witchcraft has never been my thing, I do know that it can be quite a potent force, if the practitioner has an ability.

When my mother and Aunt Sandy were little girls their father Roy had an affair.
As a family they were often short of money and their Mum (my grandmother) had to struggle to feed the girls because Grandad was often away hob-knobbing with his mistress (who was called Irene Welch) and wasn't always around to provide properly for his family.
My mother used to tell me how she and Sandy would hear Grandma crying in her room at night when Roy hadn't come home. It broke their little hearts.

One night after hearing her upset again the girls decided to do something about it. Now neither of them had had any experience or training in witchcraft at
the time. They were just little girls. My Mum was around twelve and Sandy

was about eight. They told me that they just did what they thought was "the right way", they just followed their instincts. You have to wonder what they both were in previous incarnations.

So, the while Grandma was busy in the kitchen the next afternoon. The girls sneaked off down to the end of the garden. They collected twigs and dry leaves. Bay and Sage from the herb garden. Rose petals and thistle tops. Then they lit a fire. As the flames grew and crackled and the smoke billowed out, they danced round and round, skipping and spinning, raising the energy. Then as the flames grew higher, they started to sing and chant "Irene Welch, Irene Welch, your bum will squelch, your bum will squelch." They did this until the fire had completely burned away and they flopped to the ground, worn out.

It always makes me smile to think of their loved ones and ancestors in the spirit and what they would have made of the girl's antics on that afternoon. Clearly their hocus pocus was heard by someone because their spell had real potency and proved most effective.

A day or so later, Grandad came home in a terrible state, and he poured his heart out to Grandma, not to say that he was sorry for cheating on her, but because his girlfriend Irene was very poorly. (The girls were outside and heard the conversation through an open window)

Grandma listened like the saint that she was and asked whatever had happened. "It's so awful," He sobbed. "Irene has the most awful diarrhoea. She's been taken to hospital. They're doing what they can, but they don't know why it's happening, she's dangerously dehydrated"

Grandma reassured him and said that she hoped that Irene would recover. She made him tea and gave him sympathy. (None of which he deserved). Then he wandered off, sobbing into his hanky.

My mother and Sandy were exuberant. "We've done it, we've done it "they cried.
They started to dance around chattering excitedly about how their curse had worked. Now Irene would die, and their daddy would come home and then they would be a proper family again. Suddenly their mirth was interrupted, "What's going on?" Asked Grandma. Oh Mummy" squealed the girls "We're so pleased. We made a spell to get rid of Irene. We couldn't stand to see you so upset. Now she'll die and Daddy will come home."

Grandma was horrified. "You can't do things like that. It's not right to harm people with magic, no matter what they've done." She took the girls out into the garden and showed them how to reverse the spell. To say the girls were disappointed was an understatement.

The next time Roy came to visit he told Grandma what Irene had recovered and was home. The hospital never did find out the cause of her upset tummy. But I'm pretty sure those two small girls had something to do with it.

X is for Xecotcovach

Okay this is a stretch. but it's not easy to find any paranormal words beginning with X.

An Xecotcovach is a mythical bird that comes from Mayan mythology. That's NOT what this story is about. But there's a tenuous link, and I'm going to use it.

I've always worked a lot in Wales. Often touring from town to town doing demonstrations, readings and workshops. On this occasion I was booked to work in Bridgend Spiritualist Church. Whenever I worked there I stayed with my friend Diana

Diane was a very good medium herself, and also ran a development circle. She was a very "feet on the ground" medium, and I had a lot of respect for her. You could always rely on Diane to give very honest and genuine messages.
If she told you that Grandad had said you needed to change your socks, then you definitely did.

So, Diane was running her development group one night. She was talking her group through meditation, and as is usual, she joined in herself.
Diane explained to me that as the meditation progressed, she had a vision of being in a cave that was filled with crystals of all colours. It was a massive cavern, and very beautiful. The reverie continued and as it did, she saw a figure beginning to manifest. (Remember now that this lady always said "I only do dead people. No Angels, fairies or ETs. Nothing exotic") So when she told me this story I had to laugh.

The figure continued to become clear. "It was a bird man," she told me, aghast. He was about seven feet tall. He had clawed feet, birds' legs with feathers. A man's torso and face, but the face had an eagle's beak and of course he had huge white wings (But he clearly wasn't an angel). He stood there, looking straight at her.

Cross with herself for "Imagining" such a thing, Diane called the students back. As is the norm at circles, everyone shared their experiences, except Diana, she was too angry at herself for being so ridiculous.

That night though, as she slept, she dreamed that the bird man came to her. In the dream he was talking to her (How would you even do that with a beak?) He explained that he had come to help her with her spiritual work. In the dream she was open to that, but when she woke up, she was hopping mad. She called me and had a good old rant. "What on earth is going on? I must be going mad. Things like that don't exist. I only work with dead people" she said in an exasperated tone.

I have to admit I probably wasn't much help. After all, I'd seen Troll spirits in Norway, so birdmen didn't seem too much of a stretch to me. Over the next few weeks, I received calls and texts from Diane. It seems that the birdman was quite insistent, but she did everything she could to rationalise, ignore and block him out. Then one day I received a call with a very different tone. "Ang" she uttered, "I can't believe it, but I think that the birdman is real." I could hardly believe what I was hearing, but she sounded desperate.

Diane's son was at art college, but had come home for the Easter break. She explained. "My son was in the kitchen while I was cooking breakfast. He was scribbling away at his easel, very focused, very intently. "What on earth are you drawing?" she had asked. "You seem very concentrated" "I don't know Mum" He replied. "I keep getting this image in my head. I just had to draw it, look" He turned the picture around and there it was, a drawing of the Birdman, just as Diane had seen it.

Obviously, the feathered friend had had enough of Diane's attempts to ignore him so he had found a way to convince her that he was real. In channelling a picture of himself through her son she had to admit that something was going on. As far as I know the bird-man is still with Diane and helps with lots of aspects of her spiritual work. I guess anything is possible in the spirit world.

Y is for Yoshika

So this is a strange one. (Like the others really). I think that I've mentioned before, that since my Invisible Friend came to me, he has taken me on numerous out of body trips to the Spirit World. We have been astral travelling together, to many different plains.
The first time I experienced being out of body was long before Richard first came to me.

I suppose I was around 14, so it happened around the same time that I became clairvoyant enough to start to do readings.
I can't remember what sparked it off, it just suddenly happened.
I'm sure most of you have had that feeling when you're drifting off to sleep. It's usually when you're extremely tired and fall quickly and deeply, then suddenly you jump. Sometimes that's to do the primal fight or flight reaction - but leaving your body can feel much the same.

So, on this night I came out of my body and started to fly. It was SO fast.
I remember how cold the air felt as I zoomed along. I could see the clear night sky, full of stars. I was covering so much ground. Then below I saw pine trees and could smell their strong tang. There was a house, quite a big one made of red brick.

I felt that this was Kent. I don't know why I just kind of knew. It was night-time and the house was in darkness, but there was a light on in the garage. I decided to land there. The air felt cold and when my bare feet touched the ground I could feel frost on the gravel.

The garage, like the house, was an older one. The wooden double doors were open. I stood watching and saw a vintage car with the bonnet open. A figure was half under it tinkering around. There was a radio playing quietly in the background, and I could hear the fumbling mechanic grumbling as he tried to fix his car, "Bloody thing" I heard him say. He was obviously very frustrated.

Then it dawned on me. The poor guy's day had obviously been bad enough, having to try to fix his car into the wee small hours, without me standing there like an apparition. "If he sees me here, he'll think that I'm a ghost" I realised. So I decided to leave him to it, and with that I found myself back in my body.

Most of us go wandering, in spirit form, while our physical bodies sleep.
As I've said, I've often gone on astral wanders with Richard. I'm lucky that we have such a strong connection as we've had many adventures together. He likes to show me all sorts of different things "Over there", it's very fascinating.

On one occasion he took me to see the "Check in" (as he called it).
Some vibrations in the spirit world were totally bizarre, like a Salvador Dali painting. Others are very every day, almost mundane. The levels are created by collective thought (Or so I'm told). So, for example, if enough people believe in a classic Pearly Gate, then it will have been created, and all the people with that belief may very well enter the gates of Heaven when they pass, as expected.
However, a great deal of people have never been religious, and some don't have any belief in the afterlife. So I guess that's why the "Check in" manifested.

Richard had come to me in the early hours and woken me up. He grabbed me by my wrist saying, "Hey I want to show you something," then with a swift tug he pulled me out of my body and in seconds we were flying through the air like Peter Pan and Wendy.

It wasn't long before we landed but as our feet touched the ground, I was stunned to see that we were standing in what looked like a frantically busy Heathrow Airport. (WTF?) There really were check in desks and people were queueing up. It was shockingly normal.

My face must have been a picture because Rich just burst out laughing at me. He reminded me that recently I had asked him about what happens when people pass over, and that he had explained all the different experiences that transcending souls have. I think he just decided to show me this one to blow my mind. Logically though I guess. People who have no particular beliefs, and just live normal lives, would think that an airport was okay. You just present your documents and you're sorted. and that's exactly what I was seeing, lots of spirit people of all shapes and sizes doing just that. It was the most multicultural place I had ever seen.

I remember in one corner there were several Muslim men all together on a prayer mat praying. There was a lady with a small dog on a lead asking where she should go to get her pet admitted. There was a window cleaner, still holding his ladder and bucket.

Then I noticed a tall angelic looking person, bizarrely holding a clipboard. She was talking to a confused teenage girl who was wearing jodhpurs and a hard hat. "What's happened to me?" sobbed the girl. "I remember I was riding my pony and he bucked. Now I'm here. Am I dead? "The Shining being smiled and put a hand on the teens shoulder. "Don't cry. It's not your time. Your body is in the hospital, but you will be fine. I'll send you back now" - the energy around the pair was sublime. A brilliant white cloud gently surrounded them, and when it cleared the girl was gone. No doubt now waking up in A&E.

The check-in was already quite noisy with everyone asking questions etc. Some I noticed had relatives coming to meet them. There were lots of hugs, and some tears as people who had been separated by death were suddenly back together.

Then something else caught my eye, the most amazing looking woman came striding in. She must have been seven feet tall, On her head a winged helmet. Her long hair flowed down to her waist. "Who on earth is that?" I asked, "Oh yeah right" Rich replied in his usual matter of fact way. "She's a Valkyrie. Her name is Yoshika, she has been trying to protect warriors who were fighting in conflicts. She is bringing home those who have fallen. She's honouring their bravery and sacrifice"

She turned and waved her hand in a beckoning motion. Following behind her, a small crowd of men moved forward. There were soldiers in combat gear.
A firefighter, still in uniform, dusted with soot and grease., A police officer in riot gear. They all looked tired and weary, and gazed around as if unsure what had happened to them. The Valkyrie led them onwards until they all vanished into a misty haze of swirling rainbow colours that Richard told me was the portal to the Halls of Healing.

Whenever I have travelled out of body to the spirit world I have seen the wildest things, but I will never forget those fallen heroes.

Z for Zuki

I feel like this story will seem a bit back to front. It's at the end of the book, although it happened many years ago. When my parents' rocky marriage finally ended. (Much to my relief). Mum and I moved further down into the county to a place called Carnkie, near Helston.

We had found a big old cottage called Jubilee farm. (Named after queen Victoria's Jubilee). It stood imposingly at the top of a steep hill and was surrounded by fields and moorlands. The price seemed very reasonable, so we bought it.

Right from the day we moved in things started to happen. As I've said before, my mother's side of the family were witches and mediums, so supernatural happenings were not new to us. However, future events at Jubilee farm were a whole other level.

On day one my mother and I were unpacking cutlery and dishes in the kitchen. After digging around for a while in various boxes we managed to find
some mugs, tea bags, milk and biscuits so we decided to stop for a well-earned brew.

While waiting for the kettle to boil, something strange started to happen. The milk bottle which was standing on the kitchen work surface started to move, sliding along as if it had been nudged. "Did you see that?" Mum asked.
We both agreed that we must have imagined it. It moved again, about an. Inch (WTF?). Then with a swift burst of energy the bottle shot right off the edge of the kitchen unit. It hovered in the air for a moment and then, CRASH it hit the ground, shattering glass and spraying milk everywhere. We looked at each other. Shocked.

Now this was not a good start. But we would have to make the most of things. We couldn't just run away at the first sign of spooky happenings. So we cleaned up the mess and carried on unpacking.

Next mum started arranging the dining room while I carried boxes up to my bedroom. It wasn't too long before I heard another crash and mum yelling. I rushed downstairs only to find mum with her fingers trapped in the window. She explained that she had tried to open it to let in fresh air when a force like something pushing had forced her hands down and trapped them. Now logic first. This was a very old house, so it was probably just a dodgy window. But after the milk bottle incident, we both felt uneasy. I tried to lift the window, but it was jammed fast, so mum's boyfriend Chris had to use a screwdriver to force it open. Mums' fingers were very grazed and bruised.

This was not a good start. The rest of the day went without any further misadventures, but when we finally turned in for the night, none of us were able to settle.

Over the next month's negative things continually happened and there was a lot of poltergeist activity. Objects would go missing, and then turn up in strange places. A shoe in the fridge. A hairbrush down the toilet. Doors banging in the night. Ornaments being smashed. Someone didn't want us there and was letting us know it.

One activity that the poltergeist really seemed to revel in was to change the settings on Chris's stereo. This was no ordinary sound system; it was big set up with dials like a mixing desk. It was Chris's pride and joy. He was obsessed with getting the sound exactly right. But every morning without fail, all the settings would have been changed so that the sound was totally off. Chris didn't want to believe that we had an entity in the house, so he used to accuse us of playing tricks and messing with things and it caused a lot of arguments.

We started to think that our ghost was a woman who had loved to cook because a lot of activity happened in the kitchen and was directed at mum.

On one occasion, after Sunday lunch, we were in the kitchen washing the dishes. Some cupboards were all mounted and these were where we used to put the crockery. Mum was only 5 feet tall, so had to stretch to reach the unit. As she put a plate on top of a pile of others it suddenly started to spin, like a record on a turntable. We watched in amazement. It got faster and faster and then suddenly shot out, hitting her across the arm, causing a deep gash. Blood went everywhere. Chris heard the commotion and came rushing in. He saw all the blood - and fainted. (Men) So I had to drive mum to Treliske hospital where her wound had to be stitched. I don't think the nurse believed us when we told her that this hadn't been an accident, but that a ghost had thrown a plate at mum.

At that point something had to be done. We decided to put the house back on the market, but as it would probably take time to sell, we thought we had better try to make friends with the ghost.
That evening we lit some candles and put on some ambient music. Mum burned some herbs with bay and sage, and we sat down. A few blessings were said and then we spoke to the ghost. We told her that we realised that this had been her house for a long time, but that we had bought it and were taking care of it. We had no objection to her being there, but could she please stop causing problems.
(Had these happened years to come I'm sure I would have just found it interesting, but at eighteen it was a terrifying experience).
We decided that maybe giving our ghost a name might help. We looked in a book we had of baby names. We decided on Zuki, which means beloved.

After that things started to improve. Zuki even woke us in the middle of the night when a water pipe had burst in the loft. If she hadn't done that it could have brought the ceilings down. Zuki obviously appreciated us caring for the house that she loved.

During this time my mother fell pregnant again. The pregnancy went full term but sadly, again, the baby was stillborn. She returned home. Her and Cris were both devastated. That night mum was woken up in the early hours and there, standing at the end of her bed was a woman with long braided hair, holding a baby. Mum screamed and burst into tears. The vision vanished.
I do believe that Zuki meant no harm. I think she was telling mum that she would look after her baby in the spirit world, but the whole thing just upset her more.

After that things moved quickly with the sale of Jubilee Farm and it wasn't long before we moved out. I have often cycled or driven through Carnkie over the years. Jubilee Farm always looks foreboding, as it stands alone at the top of the hill. I wonder if Zuki is still there, or if she has moved on.
But what I DO know is that that cottage has changed hands many, many times.

So to end this little book of spooky tales I thought that I would share some images. They are photos that I took which are connected to my "Tales of Treslothan" stories. Above is the Giant's Quoit. It lays at the far end of the Treslothan trail and if full of fairy energy.

The next was taken during an investigation with Joe and Lee of Frome Paranormal. We believe it to be the ghost of Lady Tryphena entering the sepulchre.

The last image is the casts that I took of the paw prints that we believe were made by the black dog. As you can see, they are bigger than my hand, and they have claws like a bear.

I hope you have enjoyed my stories and maybe you have some of your own that you would like to share.